Faulkner's Rhetoric of Loss

Faulkner's Rhetoric of Loss
A Study in Perception and Meaning

by Gail L. Mortimer

University of Texas Press, Austin

Publication of this work has been made possible in part
by a grant from the Andrew W. Mellon Foundation.

LIBRARY OF CONGRESS CATALOGING IN PUBLICATION DATA

Mortimer, Gail L. (Gail Linda), 1943–
    Faulkner's rhetoric of loss.
    Includes index.
    1. Faulkner, William, 1897–1962—Criticism and
interpretation. 2. Faulkner, William, 1897–1962—
Knowledge—Psychology. 3. Perception in literature.
4. Psychology and literature. I. Title.
PS3511.A86Z914 1983   813'.52   83–6834
ISBN 0-292-72446-2

Chapter 3 is a slightly revised version of the essay
"Significant Absences: Faulkner's Rhetoric of Loss,"
originally published in 1981 in *Novel: A Forum on
Fiction*. Grateful acknowledgment is made for permis-
sion to reprint this material.

To my mother, Laurel Mary Jerue Mortimer

Contents

Abbreviations Used

Abbreviations for works by Faulkner used in this study are listed below. Original dates of publication are indicated wherever I have used a later edition.

AA   *Absalom, Absalom!* (1936; New York: Random House, Vintage, 1972)

AILD   *As I Lay Dying* (1930; New York: Random House, Vintage, 1964)

CS   *Collected Stories of William Faulkner* (1950; New York: Random House, Vintage, 1977)

FD   *Flags in the Dust* (1973; New York: Random House, Vintage, 1974)

GDM   *Go Down, Moses* (1942; New York: Random House, Vintage, 1973)

H   *The Hamlet*, 3rd ed. (1940; New York: Random House, Vintage, 1964)

ID   *Intruder in the Dust* (New York: Random House, Modern Library, 1948)

LA   *Light in August* (1932; New York: Random House, Vintage, 1972)

M   *The Mansion* (1959; New York: Random House, Vintage, 1965)

MOS   *Mosquitoes* (1927; New York: Liveright, 1955)

R   *The Reivers: A Reminiscence* (1962; New York: New American Library, Signet, 1969)

SP   *Soldiers' Pay* (1926; New York: New American Library, Signet, 1968)

TSAF   *The Sound and the Fury* (1929; New York: Random House, Vintage, 1954)

T   *The Town* (1957; New York: Random House, Vintage, 1961)

UNV   *The Unvanquished* (1938; New York: Random House, Vintage, 1966)

WP   *The Wild Palms* (1939; New York: Random House, Vintage, 1966)

Acknowledgments

It gives me pleasure to express my appreciation to friends and colleagues who for the past several years have nourished my growing understanding of Faulkner with their encouragement and enthusiasm. I have been very grateful for the continuing support of those I studied with at the State University of New York at Buffalo: Leslie Fiedler, Murray Schwartz, Mark Shechner, Marcus Klein, Carolyn Korsmeyer, Louanne Pearson, and Beatrice Stern, all of whom showed great patience and friendship in listening to me talk—for hours at a time, it must have seemed—about Faulkner and my emerging ideas about his work. For reading and responding to parts of my work on Faulkner—and helping me to give it shape and precision—I want to thank Philip Gallagher, David Hall, Robert Esch, Lawrence Johnson, and Walter F. Taylor, Jr. For careful and generous commentary on my manuscript I am indebted to Anne Goodwyn Jones, Donald Kartiganer, Carolyn Porter, and Gerald Langford; their suggestions for improvement of the manuscript have helped to make it a tighter and more coherent argument than it might otherwise have been. I want to thank, too, four people—Walter Slatoff, John T. Irwin, David Minter, and André Bleikasten—who have written with fine insight on Faulkner and deepened my understanding of the resonances of his prose. My thanks go as well to Dennese Watts for listening and helping me to refine my thoughts, to Dean Diana Natalicio and Dean Michael Austin for their support and friendship, to Florence Dick and Helen Wheatley for typing assistance, to James Oakes for enthusiastic research assistance, and to the University Research Institute of the University of Texas at El Paso for assistance in the completion of this study. The book's errors I alone should have reason to regret; many of its strengths I owe to friends who have supported me throughout this study.

Faulkner's Rhetoric of Loss

Introduction

with nothing left, she would have to cling to that which had
robbed her, as people will   "A Rose for Emily"

Emily Grierson is only the most extreme of Faulkner's characters
who hold on fiercely to precious things that threaten to leave them.
She, of course, was doubly robbed in that her father had prevented
her from having a normal life with suitors and marriage, and then
"abandoned" her himself by dying. His putrefying corpse and,
later, that of her lover are palpable evidence of Emily's need to
deny that she has lost them. In this respect, she is like many of
Faulkner's characters, especially the brooding, introspective protagonists and the seemingly detached narrators we encounter in
most of his stories. This clinging, this holding on to things that of
their own accord would tend to go away, pervades the thinking expressed everywhere in Faulkner's prose: in his choice of individual
words, images, and themes; in the nostalgic tone of many of his
narrations and the frenetic pace of others; and in the rhetorical
structures revealing his characters' and narrators' perceptions. The
need to cling—to deny loss—is a central emotional reality underlying his fiction.

The study that follows is concerned with a broader sense of the
term "style" than that usually undertaken in literary studies. I intend to elucidate a cluster of structural idiosyncrasies in Faulkner's
descriptive passages in ways that enable us to speak profitably of a
more encompassing "perceptual style" informing his prose. One of
my basic assumptions is that a correlation exists among the various
possible human expressions of personal style. How individuals experience the world—what they see there and how they respond to
what they see—will express a particular way of being in the world.
How they focus, select, and interpret reality is biased and guided
by personal styles or personal myths. My book is an attempt to
draw connections among various rhetorical choices that Faulkner
makes—choices that we refer to collectively and recognize instinctively as his style—and to show how these choices reflect Faulk-

ner's unique ways of organizing experience. His rhetorical choices, as forms of self-expression, have psychological import. Faulkner, moreover, seems able to touch primitive regions of the imagination that are present in everyone. What we see in the perceptions this book examines is that his access to those regions is the source of much of the power of his prose.

Psychoanalytic developmental theory offers the starting point for my study of Faulkner's works. I have found that current assumptions about the formation of human identity and the emergence of human self-consciousness have suggested a variety of questions that have proven valuable in thinking about the nature of the perceptions reflected in Faulkner's prose. Those familiar with the theory will find the brief review of it that follows rather simplified, but a reiteration of some of its basic assumptions should prove helpful to others.

A number of researchers in object relations theory have focused recently on the child's awakening to the fact of its separateness from other things in the world.[1] They assume that the newborn baby experiences existence as something of a continuation of the holistic harmony of the womb and that only gradually does the child come to give up this illusion. On occasion there will be a delay between the time when the child experiences a need or wish and the time when it is filled. The *awareness* of this delay is our first subjective experience of the passage of time, and it gradually convinces us we are separate from others. The experience is assumed to be critical in our development because it involves accepting the fact we are not ominpotent (as we thought when needs and their fulfillment were experienced as coincident) and learning strategies for dealing with this new knowledge and the disappointment it brings with it. How are we led to feel our separateness? How do we experience this knowledge subjectively? How do we respond to a world now recognized as "other"? The answers to these questions involve our perceptions of and expectations about the world, whether it will meet our needs and how it will do so. The child's responses to these perceptions of what its role in the world is to be are choices that eventually contribute to the formation of its identity.

Children may adopt a variety of strategies for dealing with the frustration and rage of this period of development. This is when we become symbol-making creatures in our need to cope with disappointment. If the mother is absent, for example, a child may hum or babble to itself for comfort and to delay the panic of feeling abandoned.[2] The humming or other activity may take on a magical quality insofar as it works, that is, if it seems to lead to the mother's return. A child whose signals are never answered will have great difficulty in developing positive expectations about its environment. But the child whose mother is omnipresent may also have difficulty in that this child is not given the opportunity to realize itself as a separate being. Ideally, there is an interplay of the continuing illusion of omnipotence and gradual disillusionment so that the child learns that despite its separateness, it can influence the environment in ways that will cause its needs to be met.

Among the things a child may do to feel efficacious in these circumstances is to create what D. W. Winnicott has termed a "transitional object." Originally created as a substitute for the absent mother, this object holds value for the child because it both exists in its own right and yet is invested with the *child's* meaning: it is simultaneously self and other. It is transitional both in a spatial sense (a projection of the child's meaning out into the environment) and in a temporal one (it postpones anxiety about absent people or things). As the child plays with this object (blanket, teddy bear— something that is part of the environment, something *chosen* by the child), he or she will tend to repeat the act of sending it away and retrieving it. Like peek-a-boo and hide-and-seek, these games offer self-confidence and tolerance in encountering the absence of needed things. Every parent knows of the fierceness with which a child will insist upon complete control of the object and, paradoxically, of the seeming indifference with which it is discarded when the child has outgrown a need for it. The transitional object and playing provide a needed illusion and an opportunity to test new ideas, such as the notions of objects, their names, and the idea "away" or "gone." An individual's first utterances, too, are often attempts to link favorite objects with their absence, to reassure oneself by naming what is happening.[3] A child's capacities to name, call for, and predicate arise out of a need to anticipate—without overwhelming anxiety—the return of a loved object.

The developmental task of accommodating ourselves to our separateness can lead to a healthy sense of being independent and yet able to share and benefit from relationships with others, or it can lead to anxiety-ridden alternatives. Instead of independence, a person may experience abandonment, isolation, and panic; instead of relatedness with others, one may fear being overwhelmed or engulfed by their presence. People who have not developed relatively positive expectations about the world may cling too fiercely to people, refusing to become self-sufficient or, alternately, refusing to relate to others at all, perceiving them as indifferent, untrustworthy, or hostile.[4] What gradually develops in most of us, however, is a complex awareness both of what we can expect from the environment and of what it wants us to be and do. There is a basic orientation to the world outside ourselves that Heinz Lichtenstein has called an "identity theme."[5] All of the choices that we make about how to live our lives are based on perceptions of the world and our felt role in it; even the most diverse behaviors will be variations on a basic identity theme that may be seen as a sort of core metaphor for our existence.

Object relations theory has provided several insights that I have found significant in looking at Faulkner's works: a sense of the interplay of perception and identity in all of us; the realization that works of art are in an important sense adult, sophisticated transitional objects allowing us to create a meaningful interface between ourselves and the external world; and a sense of the psychic meanings of the rhythms of withdrawal and participation that are among the choices we make in living our lives. All three of these are fundamental to my analysis.

The identity themes for Faulkner's narrators and male characters, were we able to discover them entirely, would tend to be troubled ones, for the perceptions revealed in his descriptive passages show us that their world is experienced as unlikely to offer what they need. Instead, the central consciousness that guides us through Faulkner's fictive world assumes that precious things in that world will tend to leave it and that the only way to prevent loss is to hold on, to create containers and emphasize boundaries, to see things in ways that control the dissolution that is the normal state of things. The more nearly pathological figures in Faulkner's stories exhibit perceptual habits that reveal their worlds to be experienced as extremely hostile, threatening the loss not of some external object, but of the basic integrity of the self. This is true, as we shall see, of Joe Christmas and, in another sense, of Quentin Compson.[6] But the difference between the "average" character in Faulkner's prose and the deeply troubled one is really only a matter of degree. As we all do, characters in Faulkner's world fluctuate in their willingness to participate in the life around them. The world is perceived as tending to threaten them with the loss of precious things, on the one hand, and with being overwhelmed, on the other. They respond by perceiving things in ways that allow them to feel particular kinds of control.

The questions that I ask in looking at Faulkner's texts, questions suggested by the developmental phenomenon sketched above, have to do with the ways in which fictional perceptions evolve. I have studied descriptive passages in Faulkner's prose to understand what is being perceived, how it is being perceived, how the perception controls or structures what is seen, who is doing the seeing, and how the character responds to the perception. The devices and strategies through which Faulkner structures perceptions are especially evident when his characters are anxious about what they are encountering—as the characters defend themselves against immediate threats—but the basic forms of control can be seen throughout his fiction. The strategies I isolate are remarkably consonant with one another in generating a basic rhythm that alternates moments of control with moments in which control is relaxed: Faulkner's use of oxymora, splitting, synesthesia, and negation; his focus on boundaries or their blurring; his emphasis on the visual; his generation of images of containment or absence; his treatment of objects as traces; and his use of a figure-ground reversal technique all help to inform the perceptions in his fictive world and implicitly to interpret the nature of the world outside the self in characteristic ways.

It has been necessary occasionally to go over material familiar to critics of Faulkner—his emphasis on the past, for example—but I felt in each instance that this was necessary to establish a context from which I could go on to establish the significance of my own observations. Throughout, my concern has been to show how Faulkner's structuring of his narrators' and characters' perceptions expresses a particular way of being in the world and a particular set of expectations about that world. Whether the focus is upon metaphor, syntax, structure, or theme, Faulkner's style enacts his ongoing concern with the loss implicit in the passage of time.

I should add a word or two about the structure of my own argument. Someone once said of Faulkner that he wrote the way a dog lies down, circling, trying it, then circling some more and trying it again. In my attempt to trace the connections among the elements making up the dynamic that is my subject here, I have tended to recreate this pattern. In a number of ways, the subject matter has demanded it. The issues that I discuss are, in fact, simultaneously present, and so I have faced a difficulty analogous to that described so well by John Irwin in his introduction to *Doubling and Incest/Repetition and Revenge: A Speculative Reading of Faulkner*: presenting in a necessarily linear fashion elements which by their "simultaneous interaction . . . mutually create one another, mutually constitute themselves *as elements in a holistic structure*." [7] I have often found it necessary to defer complete consideration of one aspect of an idea until another line of thought was complete, although that element might have reinforced the meanings being discussed. As an example, the concept of figure-ground reversal recurs in several of my discussions, because there are a number of different senses in which Faulkner uses this strategy to control narrative material. None of the elements of the perceptual configuration I explore in this study exist in isolation; it is their unity of meaning that is my subject. Each chapter of the book approaches this unity from a different perspective; each, simply, asks different questions.

Chapter 1 is concerned with two intimately related and complementary issues. The chapter begins with a consideration of Joe Christmas in *Light in August*, whose precarious sense of himself is reflected narratively in exaggerated perceptions of the world around him. Another way of putting this is that he projects his deep ambivalences onto the world and then sees the world as a threatening place. In the narrative of Joe's life, we discern perceptual modalities that reflect the meaning of his confusion about who he is. Perceptions—and identity—in this novel involve the need to see women and blacks as markedly different from the self. Joe Christmas's confusion and fear are reflected in his perception of the world around him as essentially Manichaean, sharply bifurcated into self and other, good and evil, purity and corruption, male and female/black. Later in the chapter I show that Faulkner, as narrator, reinforces Joe's perceptions rhetorically by separating and isolating troublesome entities that cause his protagonist anxiety. Throughout his novels, in fact, Faulkner tends to describe any character in conflict as if he or she were really two people, or split into two characteristics (i.e., "volition" and "sentience"); this technique of splitting is central to a number of Faulkner's narrative strategies. Splitting things apart visually gives the illusion of their being under control; it avoids the need to cope with ambiguity. Yet despite these narrative expressions of control, Faulkner does not let us (or Joe) forget that vision is ultimately deceptive. For his troubled characters it is hearing and smell that tend to convey truths infallibly. The security of vision is a false security. Finally, I begin to delineate the basic thesis of my study: that such narrative strategies are characteristic of a dynamic oscillation between relaxation and control that informs much of Faulkner's prose, that he has characteristic ways of implying control even as he undermines the security he tries to create for his characters. Faulkner's world is a world sustained among tensions about loss: loss of the self, loss of control, loss of desired objects through the passage of time.

Chapter 2 considers the characteristic ways in which Faulkner describes objects and activities that exist through the course of time. Beleaguered as his characters are with a constant awareness of change, Faulkner narratively reflects the anxiety of such an awareness by, on the one hand, relying on vision to make things cohere and stay the same and, on the other, undermining perceptions with the obliquity of his descriptions and otherwise implying that objects are dissolving or fading even as he tries to capture them in language. Faulkner exploits Bergson's notion of the way we habitually break the fluidity of reality into manageable and finite "pictures" that offer us reference points from which to act. The insights of Bergson helped Faulkner decide on indirect descriptive approaches: he tends to use motion to speak of stasis, stasis to speak of motion. The concept of figure-ground reversal helps us to see the strengths and subtleties of this narrative indirection. Faulkner grapples in these descriptions with the notion of identity through time—how it is that objects remain the same and yet change as time passes. It is the temporal counterpart of the problem of identity he confronted in the story of Joe Christmas, and again the problem of identity is confluent with the problem of the narrative presentation of perceptions. Faulkner's descriptions of objects in time suggest his notion that simple cohesiveness keeps objects intact; on their own, they would tend to lose their identity, to flow into one another, or back into the basic elements of earth and water. Objects' susceptibility to change through time is reflected visually as they fragment and dissolve before our eyes; sight simply fails to control perceptions in satisfactory ways. Characters preoccupied (as so many of Faulkner's are) with the effects of time's passage find that their very perceptions reflect a blurring of boundaries that is a loss of control. A failure of vision to make things remain the same and a failure of things to retain their identity are correlates throughout Faulkner's stories.

Chapter 3 is a discussion of Faulkner's dualistic depiction of the past and the relation of this phenomenon to his creation of absences of all sorts in his stories. Absence enters the world, and our consciousness, at precisely the moment we become aware of the passage of time. It is, as I have said, the occasion for our becoming symbolizing beings. Faulkner's rhythmic oscillation between seeing the past as pervading and informing every present moment and seeing it as separate and importantly other involves the same rhythm of flowing and control that I discuss in chapters 1 and 2 as it is found in more easily recognizable descriptions. Objects present in Faulkner's world tend to be traces of absent things, significant less in themselves than by virtue of what they say about those absent things. Faulkner also undermines our belief that we can *know*, and thus feel in some control of, the past by using oxymoronic structures, "either/or" and "neither/nor" constructions, and negation in ways that confuse our perceptions and call into question the very narrative he is relating. And he uses images of containers and absences to convey his characters' anxiety in the face of loss: by focusing on what has just been lost, by creating images of emptiness and then only partially filling them, by playing with the notion of crossing forbidden boundaries (conceptual, social, narrative), and by implying that the importance of words and things resides in their function as symbols of absent things. In all of these narrative choices, we see a fundamental preoccupation with a world of loss and a response to it that involves rhythmic movements between being in and with that world of loss, flowing with it and experiencing its flux, and, alternately, denying it by asserting control over the perceptions that otherwise convey anxiety. This is a way of seeing things that all of Faulkner's introspective protagonists share to some degree. In characters such as Quentin Compson, intense rhetoric exacerbates our sense that their blurred and distorted perceptions mirror a universe that denies most of what we ask of it.

In chapter 4 I suggest one final variation on the rhythm of flowing and control that characterizes so many of Faulkner's rhetorical strategies: the interplay of ritual and myth. In Faulkner's stories, as in our cultural experience, ritual tends to consist of controlled interactions between groups or things that would otherwise occasion anxiety; myth is the meaning that we discover in those actions, as well as the meaning out of which they are born. Faulkner's characters enact rituals when encountering threatening things; they hope by performing them correctly to undo the effects of time, the sequence of events that have made the object of the ritual threatening in the first place. With nature, especially the wilderness, with blacks, and with women, Faulkner's protagonists attempt ritualistically to make their encounters predictable. Sometimes they succeed, but never with women. This suggests that the deepest disease in Faulkner's fictive world is a dis-ease with women, a basic conviction of their threatening otherness, their ineluctable alienation. When rituals do work, characters may experience a transcendence of the occasion of the ritual, a transcendence of time. They feel safe for one brief moment, beyond the need for control. Some of Faulkner's characters even seem to embody the ability to transcend a preoccupation with time, born of their essential difference from the Southern white male who is the central consciousness of his stories. Blacks (in certain circumstances), people like Sam Fathers and Lucas Beauchamp, women, and mules all share a natural indifference to the tormenting passage of time—in the eyes, that is, of the Faulknerian consciousness through which we know his novels. His protagonists, in contrast, figures such as Joe Christmas, Horace Benbow, Bayard Sartoris, and the schoolteacher Labove, enact rituals that end simply as repeated obsessive behavior; even the "transcendence" they sometimes achieve is a perverse one, for it is a moment of freedom found in final despair, death, or castration.

In his important new biography of Faulkner, David Minter attempts to articulate some of the deep and pervasive reciprocities between Faulkner's life and work. He reaches a number of conclusions remarkably consistent with my own exploration of Faulkner's texts. I have not, as Minter has done, drawn many correspondences between Faulkner's fictional experiments and his life since I intend my focus to be literary analysis rather than psychobiography. I have no doubt that there *are* important correlations between the two, but I suspect that many of them are finally irrecoverable. My own concern here has been to explicate the quality of the consciousness that informs Faulkner's fiction, the cluster of perceptual habits that his characters and narrators share, and the way of being in the world that is reflected in both the form and content of his stories. I suspect that the true relationship between Faulkner's life and his writing involved the fictional universe allowing him to project aspects of his own experience into a medium and an occasion in which he could play with them imaginatively. As Minter puts it, "To create meant presenting an image of life as it was, modified by life as it 'should have been.'" [8] It seems likely, too, that the writing enabled Faulkner to deal creatively with troubling thoughts and thus return to life with greater hope. Certainly literary history offers us an extraordinary number of instances wherein authors' lives collapsed in some crucial way when they could no longer transmute parts of their experience into art. It is clear from Minter's book that neither life alone nor art alone was enough for Faulkner: "Both of his worlds seemed to him to possess not only a promise of life but a threat of impoverishment, even extinction. It was, therefore, in oscillation that he saw possibility. To him each world was the only sufficient cure for the other. If one called him to imaginative flights or dives, and promised him harmony and control, the other called him to a kind of empirical gaiety, and promised him variety and change. His deepest recognition was the need both his life and his art had of both the flights and the gaiety." [9]

But apart from the important correlations between Faulkner's personal life and those of his characters, so emphasized by Minter, the two realms are distinct. Faulkner's personal life became highly stylized, but in his fiction, he took chances. Minter tells us that "although [Faulkner] continued to seek a formal, ceremonial life, he experimented in art with the dissolution of everything: one part of the radically venturesome quality of his writing derives from his willingness to brave the loss of all familiar procedures and the disintegration of all familiar forms." [10] It is this experimentation with "the dissolution of everything" that first fascinated me about Faulkner and led me to ask questions from the point of view of how perceptions in his fiction evolve, how they are structured, how they control what is perceived. Perhaps the insight I share most strongly with David Minter is that of the basic role of rhythms or oscillations between possibilities in Faulkner's imagination. Minter finds them in Faulkner's alternation between participation in and withdrawal from life whereas I see them as pervading his rhetorical strategies. I use Minter's observations throughout my study, although most frequently in notes, because of the consistency with which, though asking different questions, we approach the same truths.

In only one case have I chosen to talk about the correspondences between Faulkner's life and his writing in any depth—in my discussion of his thoughts about women. Minter agrees that the role of women is crucial; he writes of *Light in August*: "Never before had Faulkner made so clear the relation he sensed between a man's attitude toward women and his disposition toward life." [11] I think the texts disclose a fundamental and unresolved ambivalence toward women that is basic to most of the perceptual gestalts I have isolated. Thus, in my final chapter, I show that Faulkner's characters experience the severest helplessness and greatest anxiety when they are with women, that they have projected their gravest fears onto women in ways that parallel the most basic perceptions structuring their lives.

Chapter One
Identity and the Spatial Imagination

his own flesh as well as all space was still a cage
Light in August, p. 151

The nature of human identity is a pivotal issue in Faulkner's *Light in August*, which explores the anguish of a man who can neither know himself nor find acceptance with others because of the ambiguity surrounding who he is. Joe Christmas's problem is not the fact of the presence or absence of Negro blood in his body. His tragedy, as Faulkner expressed it, is "not to know what he is and to know that he will never know."[1] It is Joe's *sense* of self as he observes both himself and how others behave toward him that is in jeopardy, and the precariousness of his sense of identity pervasively influences his behavior and his perceptions.[2] His difficulties are exacerbated because Joe lives in the early twentieth-century South, an environment committed to defining its people precisely in terms of their race and committed, therefore, to repudiating the possibility of ambiguity about one's "blackness" or "whiteness." In his attempts to define himself, Joe is doomed by his own internal ambivalence about who he might be and by the rigidity of others' responses to him. In the narrative development of his story, however, we find a configuration of perceptual habits that suggest the basis of his confusion as well as of the inordinate need of Faulkner's South to maintain a fixed distinction between blacks and whites.

Faulkner's own identity as the descendant of a Southern aristocratic family is important because the consciousness of "the Southern aristocrat *manqué*"[3] provides the perceptual reference point from which we can understand why things in Faulkner's world are viewed as they are. Whether we speak of Faulkner's narrators or his characters, the central consciousness in his fiction is always one which sees the Southern gentleman as the self and experiences others as being markedly different from that self. Depending upon the circumstances of a particular character, he will see the

Other as including such figures as women, blacks, Yankees, and of course the Snopeses. In this novel about a protagonist whose identity remains in doubt, the urgency of the need to keep these Others separate from the self is especially evident. Joe Christmas's psychological preoccupation is reflected narratively as Faulkner isolates a set of emotionally compelling characteristics and the figures with whom they are identified. The language he uses in doing so is emotionally overcharged, as if to emphasize Joe's compelling need to be constantly aware of the otherness of figures who threaten his attempts at autonomy.

Human identity, as I suggested in the Introduction, is one of the relatively stable products emerging from our earliest conceptual task, learning to recognize and be more or less comfortable with our separate existence in the world. It seems likely that this early experience, complicated and subtle at best, would be especially complex in the Southern culture into which Faulkner was born. Instead of a single maternal figure guiding a child to a sense of separateness and identity, the Southern child was often raised alongside Negro (and white) siblings by a black, as well as a white, mother. In this context, the complicated sorting out of one's self as a being with a coherent and clear identity of one's own might well be made more difficult by the presence of two maternal figures and two races.[4] Obviously, the young child is not aware of racial biases or fears, but it seems likely that later, socially imposed learning about the "meaning" of the races would, in retrospect, occasion a good deal of confusion because of this closeness to a black (as well as a white) mother and siblings. This would be especially true if the child has been fed (or nursed), washed, disciplined, and loved by the black mother, early physical intimacies that engender the child's first experience of love. In a meaningful emotional sense, if a white child is nursed and raised by a black woman, the white mother may be felt to be absent. In *The Sound and the Fury* Caroline Compson is portrayed as such an absent figure, aloof and egoistic to such a degree that her sons turn to their sister Caddy for nurturance and love.[5] Although Faulkner's own mother was not absent in precisely this way when he was an infant, his texts suggest that he assimilated this aspect of the Southern mythos, as he did so many others, and made it part of his vision of Southern life. Moreover, his devotion to his second mother, "Mammy Callie" (Caroline Barr), who joined his family when he was five, was unmistakable.[6] *Go Down, Moses*, an extended study of blacks' treatment in the South, is dedicated to her, Faulkner tells us, in gratitude for her faithfulness and "immeasurable devotion and love."

The white male child in turn-of-the-century, small-town Southern society was faced with lessons about the black race and about women that seem likely to have been emotionally bewildering. Taught through socialization of various sorts that women and blacks were inferior to him, he would feel the lesson contradicted by his vivid early experience of their closeness and love—and thus their potency in his life. They are the people with whom he spends nearly all of his early life, not the relatively absent father, and yet society expects him to assert himself as their proper guide and authority, to dominate them if necessary. Setting himself apart from them and finding an appropriate (white male) person to identify with would, in such circumstances, become important steps in establishing a viable sense of identity within a racist and sexist society.

Faulkner himself poignantly expressed the pain of the Southern child who breaks away from Negro siblings with whom he had been raised. In "The Fire and the Hearth" Carothers Edmonds destroys his rapport with his black foster brother Henry by snubbing him; then, in despair, he realizes that he cannot undo it, that he has received "the old curse of his fathers, the old haughty ancestral pride" that will separate him permanently from Henry (GDM 111). As he thinks back to the similar pasts of his and Henry's fathers, who also shared their infancy, Edmonds conveys a sense of the emotional significance of having had a black mother: "it never even occurred to him that they in their turn and simultaneously had not had *the first of remembering* projected upon a single woman whose skin was likewise dark" (GDM 110, emphasis mine).

David Minter writes that the moment signalling "the end of childhood and the beginning of awareness . . . possessed particular poignancy for [Faulkner]."[7] To be born into awareness is to be deprived forever of the childhood illusion of benevolence and peace: "The deep nostalgia that informs so much of his fiction is often associated . . . with loss of childhood—that is, a world prior to disappointment, division, bitterness, a world not yet in need of facelifting."[8] About Faulkner's childhood, Minter concludes that during "his earliest years he experienced an unusually strong sense of holistic unity with his family, and especially with his mother. From these years, he gathered a sense of his world as blessed and of himself as virtually omnipotent. Although he suffered no great trauma, he lost this double sense of well-being at an early age, and he found the experience painful. Troubled in part by the loss itself and in part by the feeling that those who had bequeathed blessedness had also destroyed it, he emerged from childhood determined to control his relations to his world."[9] Faulkner shares with his characters a profound ambivalence born in a sense of loss of well-being, and, like them, he experienced much of this ambivalence as a "deep, varied dis-ease with women" and a strong distrust of them.[10]

In Faulkner's stories the black person and the female evoke strikingly similar emotions in characters to whom they represent all that is "other" than the self. Defending against a closeness (= attraction = dependence) to them that feels personally threatening, the white male secures his sense of self only by repeatedly denying his ambivalence toward them, by asserting his autonomy.[11] Consequently, while responses to particular black people and women will vary, the figure who consistently generates the most violent and immediate anxiety in Joe Christmas and others among Faulkner's male characters is the "womanshenegro" (LA 147).[12] She is somehow the embodiment of all threats to his well-being, threats born in a psychic time when he felt helpless and she seemed omnipotent. Faulkner's personal mythology appears to have included some of these feelings as well. Joseph Blotner has quoted Sherwood Anderson's criticism of Faulkner's "pernicious Southern attitudes": "I remember, when I first met him, when he had first come from his own little Southern town, sitting with him one evening before the cathedral in New Orleans while he contended with entire seriousness that the cross between the white man and the Negro woman always resulted, after the first crossing, in sterility. He spoke of the cross between the jack and the mare that produced the mule and said that, as between the white man and the Negro woman, it was just the same."[13] Faulkner seems to have been telling tall tales here; he loved, as we know, to put things over on people. But apart from the overt content of the anecdote, it corroborates an element in Faulkner's imagination that insists on the separation of the white male from the figure who is most strongly experienced as alien, as other.

The association between the Black and the Female [14] is basic to Faulkner's vision, and he invariably depicts blackness as something one gets from one's mother. Historically and sociologically, of course, this rings true. In Faulkner's South, it was—for obvious reasons—far more likely that a white man would force his sexual attentions on a black woman than otherwise. Consequently, before abolition the race of one's mother nearly always determined whether or not a person was a slave. The *imaginative* association of the two figures and their assumed characteristics, however, obtains in many of Faulkner's stories even when he might have tried out other fictional possibilities. Virtually the only exception is Joe Christmas, whose blackness through his father is precisely what remains in doubt.

In his search for a stable identity, Joe Christmas does not find it possible to live with both possibilities, that he is black and that he is white, because society possesses clearly delineated and irreconcilable expectations about how, in either case, he must behave. As a Southern child who experiences in himself the disparate qualities attributed to the two races and who tries to create a wholeness of self based in his recognition of these qualities, he has no model in whom he can see them integrated, no one with whom to "identify." Joe's emotional sense of himself, then, is continually at odds with society's demands of him. Not knowing who he is in such circumstances leads inevitably to ambivalence about the very things he comes to recognize as "self." For Joe and for others, as psychoanalyst Phyllis Greenacre points out, an individual's sense of identity is far from being autonomous: "in general a sense of identity involves some relation to others and has a socially determined component, with a degree of observation both by the person himself and/or through another person. Even for the individual, his inner sense of himself is not enough to produce a sense of identity. . . . The sense of the self-image [the core of awareness around which one's sense of identity is built] is maintained and perhaps vitalized by the continual redefinement which accompanies comparison and contrast with others." [15]

Joe is sent by Doc Hines, his fanatical grandfather, to a white children's orphanage, where he is gradually led to believe that he is black. Thus, his personal history forces upon him particular feelings of inferiority, guilt, and self-hatred. The emotional complexity of his early life assures that he will never achieve a coherent sense of himself and encourages his unusually intense struggle to create a sense of identity that will be as self-sufficient as possible. As we shall see, Joe's confused perceptions of himself prevent him from simply choosing to live as either a white or a black man, and they are increasingly reflected in his perceptions of the world around him.

In thinking about Joe's ways of seeing those around him— ways that explicitly reflect his confusions about his own identity— we must begin with Lena Grove, who is a foil for Joe throughout *Light in August*.[16] Lena is the archetypal female, the serene woman, at home with nature, with the earth, with birth, with her own physical self, with the mysterious source of life. Faulkner specifically and repeatedly associates her with food and pregnancy (thus, full of life and life processes), with acceptance (of life, food, people as they are), with intuition, motionlessness, timelessness (mechanical time has no relevance for her), and with feeling at home in general. Joe never encounters Lena, but it becomes clear that in his own associations the female (of which Lena is the quintessence) connotes blackness or darkness and its dangers, the body (physical self), fecundity, softness, wetness, warmth, blood, smothering, secretiveness, smells, and sensuality.

An early experience at the orphanage prefigures the cluster of associations and feelings that become characteristic of Joe in his relationships with women. Specifically, his fears about the female are related to his sense that his bodily boundaries are in jeopardy and that he will be engulfed by her or otherwise be destroyed. This is forecast in his eating, vomiting, and confusion while hidden in the dark in the dietician's room. All of the women in Joe's life bring with them specifically oral threats: Miss Atkins, the dietician; Bobbie Allen, a waitress; and Mrs. McEachern and Joanna Burden, who try to feed him. Whenever Joe must come to terms with something in himself that reminds him of the feminine—for example, his own physical nature, dependent on food and sleep—he is forced to face the implications of all that the feminine threatens. In a number of scenes, for example, he violently throws food away rather than accept it from a woman (LA 145, 224–225). These are vulnerable moments, when he believes that to accept food is to be entrapped and to lose his cherished (if tenuous) autonomy. Joe is to be compared with Lena in her calm acceptance of food and resting place, even from strangers, as if she simply knows, without surprise, that she will be taken care of.[17]

Through Joe's relationships with women, Faulkner sets up a polarity of ideas, one group representing the female, suggested above, and the other representing the male *as he comes to terms with the female or "otherness" of existence.* It is a remarkable bifurcation of possible ways of being in the world. Faulkner treats them as mutually exclusive states of being between which Joe oscillates in his futile attempts to feel whole and to create a viable sense of himself. Like many of Faulkner's male characters,[18] Joe is characterized by his alienation from nature and natural processes, his penchant for cleanliness, his aloneness and isolation, his motion and struggle, and his feeling bound by time and space. Joe is associated in the novel with whiteness or lightness, with an absence of food through his rejection of it or abstinence, with the odorless and the bodiless (transcendence of the physical), with taking rather than accepting—in short, with the qualities that would seem to assure autonomy.

This duality, which pervades Faulkner's descriptive passages in this and a number of his other novels, can help us to understand the affective quality of much of his fiction. The serenity and timelessness surrounding Lena's travels in search of Lucas Burch, for example, reveal her feminine stasis and comfortableness in the world, but they also reflect an effortless mobility that brings into vivid contrast Joe's own experience of the "open road." While Lena is carried along by wagons described in homely metaphors, "like a shabby bead upon the mild red string of road," and the road itself rolls along "like already measured thread being rewound onto a spool" (LA 6), Joe feels himself driven along alien, circular roads that lead him back inexorably to his fate, to the givens of his existence: "But I have never got outside that circle. I have never broken out of the ring of what I have already done and cannot ever undo" (LA 321). To Lena the past is "a peaceful corridor paved with unflagging and tranquil faith" (LA 4), but for Joe "all the past was a flat pattern . . . all that had ever been was the same as all that was to be, since tomorrow to-be and had-been would be the same" (LA 266).[19] These words reflect both an absence of progress and the perception of life as a single, problematic dilemma—a struggle against entrapment.[20]

The stick still fell; as the progress of the horse slowed, the speed of the stick increased in exact ratio. But the horse slowed, sheering into the curb. Joe pulled at its head, beating it, but it slowed into the curb and stopped, shadowdappled, its head down, trembling, its breathing almost like a human voice. Yet still the rider leaned forward in the arrested saddle, in the attitude of terrific speed, beating the horse across the rump . . . they might have been an equestrian statue strayed from its pedestal and come to rest . . . (LA 196–197)

Furious activity that gets him nowhere is set in opposition to serene, unquestioning progress; inexorable, time-bound fate is set against a timeless peacefulness. This distinction between Joe and Lena emphasizes Joe's continual attitude of flight, his Gothic sense of being-in-the-world.[21]

Joe's demoniacal drivenness and alienation from both nature and society reflect his inner flight from ambiguities within himself. His development, as Faulkner carefully chronicles it, pivots on his basic awareness of being different. Joe does not know who Doc Hines is or that he is his grandfather, but as a child he is continually aware that Hines is staring at him, setting him apart from the other children at the orphanage. The other children, moreover, probably at Hines's instigation, taunt Joe by calling him "nigger." In these events Faulkner shows that Joe is being led to see "blackness" as an inextricable part of his self-definition, as a trait that is simultaneously "self" and "other."

Even as a very young child, Joe stays away from the other children, as if to acknowledge their judgment of him. His withdrawal and vulnerability exacerbate the massive disorientation (characterized by boundary chaos) he feels when he becomes sick in the dietician's closet and when he tries to deal with her undefined anger. This is the paradigm for his feelings about being black and shamed and his lifelong flirtation with punishment. At the moment Joe expects physical punishment from the dietician, indeed hopes for it to relieve his guilt, she hurls at him *in its place* the definition he is coming to believe about himself: "You little nigger bastard!" (LA 114). To be crouched in "rife, pinkwomansmelling" clothes and shoes (LA 114), to be eating, sweating, and vomiting in the dark, to experience physical terror followed by an even more terrifying absence of tangible punishment—these injuries intensify Joe's insecurity and focus it into oral and boundary dilemmas whenever he confronts women.

Thinking in such terms, we are able to understand much of what happens in Joe's later life. It is precisely the feminine which he cannot assimilate and yet which confronts him as an aspect of his own identity. Time after time we see him running from the black/body/woman/filth/animal parts of himself: "On all sides, *even within him*, the bodiless fecundmellow voices of negro women murmured. It was as though he and all other manshaped life about him had been returned to the lightless hot wet primogenitive Female. He began to run . . . toward the next street lamp . . . the cold hard air of white people" (LA 107, emphasis mine).

Indeed, Joe's conflicted identity is so tenuous that he is sometimes in doubt that he even exists,[22] and he is led into sexual and aggressive behavior primarily to have his own existence affirmed by others. He often wills his own punishment and initiates violence in others; he is only apparently the victim. His responses to such encounters confirm that some need of his has been filled: "When the strap fell he did not flinch, no quiver passed over his face. He was looking straight ahead, with a rapt, calm expression like a monk in a picture. McEachern began to strike methodically, with slow and deliberate force, still without heat or anger. It would have been hard to say which face was the more rapt, more calm, more convinced" (LA 140).[23] And again, a few pages later: "Perhaps the boy knew that he already held the strap in his hand. It rose and fell, deliberate, numbered, with deliberate, flat reports. The boy's body might have been wood or stone; a post or a tower upon which the sentient part of him mused like a hermit, contemplative and remote with ecstasy and selfcrucifixion. . . . He felt like an eagle: hard, sufficient, potent, remorseless, strong" (LA 150). The man beating him is Simon McEachern, his adopted father, whose inexorable code of behavior offers a semblance of stability in Joe's life by systematically affirming—through literally beating him—his autonomous existence.[24] "Perhaps he was thinking then how he and the man could always count upon one another, depend upon one another; that it was the woman alone who was unpredictable" (LA 149).

Faulkner's men perceive women as being unpredictable creatures by virtue of their softness, their secretiveness, and their in-

stinctive knowledge of evil. Woman after woman in Faulkner's stories is described in such terms by narrators and characters alike.
Because she is female, the dietician has a "natural female infalli-
bility for the spontaneous comprehension of evil" (LA 117). Joe
thinks of Mrs. McEachern: "It was the woman who, with a woman's affinity and instinct for secrecy, for casting a faint taint of evil
about the most trivial and innocent actions" (LA 157); "It was she
who trusted him, who insisted on trusting him as she insisted on
his eating: by conspiracy, in secret . . ." (LA 158); "It was the
woman: that soft kindness which he believed himself doomed to be
forever victim of . . ." (LA 158). Joanna Burden, like the women
in Joe's life before her, insists upon secrets: "She revealed an unex-
pected and infallible instinct for intrigue. She insisted on a place
for concealing notes, letters. It was in a hollow fence post below the
rotting stable . . . sometimes he would have to seek her about the
dark house until he found her, hidden, in closets, in empty rooms,
waiting . . ." (LA 245). Quentin Compson in *The Sound and the
Fury* typifies in his tormented perceptions this male mystification
in the presence of female ineffability, which men experience as in-
sidiousness: "*Women are like that they dont acquire knowledge of people we are for that they are just born with a practical fertility of suspi-
cion that makes a crop every so often and usually right they have an
affinity for evil for supplying whatever the evil lacks in itself for drawing
it about them instinctively as you do bedclothing in slumber fertilising
the mind for it until the evil has served its purpose whether it ever existed
or no*" (TSAF 119).

For Joe Christmas the secret that initiates women into their
special knowledge is the horror, for him, of menstruation. One of
the boys Joe knew "drew a picture, physical, actual, to be dis-
cerned by the sense of smell and even of sight. It moved them: the
temporary and abject helplessness of that which tantalised and
frustrated desire; the smooth and superior shape in which volition
dwelled doomed to be at stated and inescapable intervals victims of
periodical filth" (LA 173). The sense of smell is decisive as men in
Faulkner's world feel threatened, because it—like menstruation
and like women themselves—is secretive and insidious. When you
are aware of it, a smell is no longer safely outside of you but instead
is mixed up with you, inside, neither locatable nor controllable,
and no longer "other." It is too late to do anything; you feel infil-
trated, smothered. Even as Mrs. McEachern tries to save Joe from

punishment and to smuggle food into his room, she is seen as an intruder: "both the man and the boy accepting [the punishment] as a natural and inescapable fact until she, getting in the way, *must give it an odor*, an attenuation, and aftertaste" (LA 157, emphasis mine).

Consequently, it is not simply the "womanshenegro" I mentioned earlier but the smell ineluctably confirming the presence of a threat that causes Faulkner's male characters to defend themselves vehemently: "[Joe] entered the shed. It was dark. At once he was overcome by a terrible haste. There was something in him trying to get out, like when he had used to think of toothpaste. But he could not move at once, standing there, smelling the woman, smelling the negro all at once; enclosed by the womanshenegro and the haste, driven, having to wait . . ." (LA 146–147). Immediately thereafter, Joe is involved in a fight with the boys who have come to the shed with him. Soon, "he still struggled, fighting, weeping. There was no She at all now. They just fought; it was as if a wind had blown among them, hard and clean" (LA 147). Such associations are ubiquitous in Faulkner's stories: the sense of smell tells you whether you are in a safe place or, near women, in danger. Faulkner's men tend to love the smell of horses: "[Joe] was thinking now, aloud now, 'Why in hell do I want to smell horses?' Then he said, fumbling: 'It's because they are not women. Even a mare horse is a kind of man'" (LA 101). When Eula Varner comes to Gavin Stevens's office, then, implicitly offering herself to this man who has longed for her for years, the threat that she represents becomes palpable: "[She was] still not moving: just standing there facing me so that what I smelled was not even just woman but that terrible, that drowning envelopment" (T 95).

When Joe learns about menstruation, he copes with it in a manner typical of Faulkner's men in relating to women or to nature—he performs a ritual: "he shot a sheep. . . . Then he knelt, his hands in the yet warm blood of the dying beast, trembling, dry-mouthed, backglaring" (LA 174); "With the slain sheep he had bought immunity . . ." (LA 176).

Faulkner's dualistic world is ultimately Manichaean. The feminine/black association with evil and the insidious is perpetually at odds with what a man can know or be comfortable with. The evils of the flesh remain intrinsic to woman, who both attracts and repels. Hers is the "smooth and superior shape" (LA 173) to which

Faulkner often alludes in one of his favorite metaphors, the urn: "[Joe] reached the woods and entered . . . he seemed to see a diminishing row of suavely shaped urns in moonlight, blanched. And not one was perfect. Each one was cracked and from each crack there issued something liquid, deathcolored, and foul. He touched a tree, leaning his propped arms against it, seeing the ranked and moonlit urns. He vomited" (LA 177–178).[25]

Joe Christmas's relationships with women, as I have suggested, force him to confront his own racial and sexual ambiguities. His sexual encounters are always followed by a frantic affirmation of his separateness. It is as if the closeness has mobilized fears of engulfment and confusion about where he stops and she begins: "beneath the dark and equivocal and symbolical archways of midnight he bedded with the women and paid them when he had the money, and when he did not have it he bedded anyway and then told them that he was a negro" (LA 211). This announcement leads quickly to violence, a cursing or a beating. But on one occasion this tactic does not work:

> He rose from the bed and told the woman that he was a
> negro. "You are?" she said. "I thought maybe you were just
> another wop or something." She looked at him, without par-
> ticular interest; then she evidently saw something in his face
> . . . she began to move backward slowly before him, staring
> at him, her face draining, her mouth open to scream. Then
> she did scream. It took two policemen to subdue him. At
> first they thought that the woman was dead.
> He was sick after that. . . . He stayed sick for two years.
>
> (LA 211–212)

Joe experiences this woman's indifference to his identity as negation, as a refusal to recognize his distinctiveness as a separate human being. She has implied that Joe's identity, whose establishment and reinforcement are the constant motive for his behavior, does not matter. As Joe expresses it to Joanna Burden, "If I'm not [Negro], damned if I haven't wasted a lot of time" (LA 241). His beating of the prostitute and of others in the course of the novel (Lucas Burch, Joanna Burden) is another reflection of his need to provoke a response or affirmation in others.[26] Like his masochism, Joe's sadism reassures him that he is a person separate from (not engulfed or overwhelmed by) other human beings.

For the most part Joe's body bogs him down, inhibits his movement, and seems a gross reminder of his dependence and vulnerability. The only time in the novel when he seems close to finding the peace he seeks is when he has been in the countryside, away from people, for a week: ". . . as he walks steadily on, he thinks that this is what it is—the looking and seeing—which gives him peace and unhaste and quiet, until suddenly the true answer comes to him. He feels dry and light. 'I dont have to bother about having to eat anymore,' he thinks. 'That's what it is'" (LA 320). His body's need for rest, for food, and for women endangers the autonomous, nearly bodiless existence we see him striving toward so often in his fasting and lonely vigils. After he has been close to a woman, Joe creates a distance from her (1) to eliminate the panic of closeness and to reestablish his separateness, and (2) to overcome even his own body by detachedly being aware of it. Joe usually achieves this detachment only after pain of some sort (when one's surfaces feel very tangible), as we have seen when he is beaten. The threat represented by women, however, is so treacherous that even this response may be ineffectual, and the second, nymphomaniacal phase of his relationship with Joanna is described specifically in terms of engulfment: "as though he had fallen into a sewer" (LA 242); "he found her, hidden, in closets, in empty rooms, waiting, panting, her eyes in the dark glowing like the eyes of cats" (LA 245); "with her wild hair, each strand of which would seem to come alive like octopus tentacles, and her wild hands and her breathing: 'Negro! Negro! Negro!'" (LA 245); "He began to be afraid. He could not have said of what. But he began to see himself as from a distance, like a man being sucked down into a bottomless morass" (LA 246).

Joe Christmas believes irreconcilable facts about himself,[27] that he is black and not black, woman and not woman, somewhere at the center of his being. His macabre death, ironically, releases him from the feminine and all other fleshliness in himself, his own "pent black blood," in what appears to be a grotesque parody of his fears of destruction: castration itself; the mocking resemblance of his wound to menstruation, which so appalls him; and a rhetoric that insists upon rising, sexual, male power precisely when it has become impossible: "upon that black blast [the rush of blood] the man seemed to rise soaring into their memories forever and ever" (LA 440). This vision of transcending his body, of being freed from it, parallels other occasions in the novel (beatings, fasting) when Joe conquers, however briefly, the encumbrance of a body that sabotages his efforts to achieve a stable identity and peace for himself: ". . . his own flesh as well as all space was still a cage" (LA 151).

Virtually all of the elements of Joe's personality are clarified when we recognize this flight from something threatening at the center of the self: his passivity and exhilaration when he is beaten, his Calvinistic unyieldingness, his latent homosexuality and his disgust with the palpably feminine (his women are each in some respect masculine figures), and his self-exposure both in exhibitionism and in surrendering to punishment. Each of his actions reflects a preoccupation with boundaries, that is, with keeping things separate that tend to fuse: "He watched his body grow white out of the darkness like a kodak print emerging from the liquid" (LA 100). Being ashamed, Joe is concerned with the basis of that shame. It remains elusive, subsumed vaguely under the term "blackness," his apparent Negro blood. The scene at the orphanage has proven paradigmatic; the pattern of his life is to seek punishment to relieve the anxiety of a guilt whose source he cannot locate. The Calvinism of Joe's persecutors, who believed in being "chosen" and in predestination, reinforces the impression that his guilt/blood has been imposed on him by unknown powers. In a sense, this alien part of himself is experienced as a de facto engulfment which he must, paradoxically, both deny and prevent from happening again in order to retain his sense of identity.

For Joe and for Faulkner, the male and the female are not principles that can be integrated to create wholeness within the personality, as Jung, for example, saw them.[28] Instead, they remain forever alien to one another. There are characters in Faulkner's stories whom we experience initially as rich, full, and integrated with the life around them, but it is never the genuine fusion of the creative possibilities symbolized by the male and the female in each of us. Lena Grove, Eula Varner, and others like them are women whose plenitude is a function of their immersion in the physical, sensual, and natural aspects of life; they seem, however, to have no cerebral, spiritual, or moral existence as do the young, tormented men who are the protagonists of so many of Faulkner's novels. Consequently, readers have often felt that these women are not fully developed or viable figures. Lena and Dewey Dell have been called "stupid," and Faulkner's portrayal of Eula seems like a caricature in its insistence that she is a distillation of all sexuality in a single body. To different degrees, these women are embodiments of the female, an abstraction that hovers like a Platonic form over Faulkner's universe. A few other figures, such as Isaac McCaslin and Sam Fathers, are rich figures because they have successfully established a rapport with the natural world. In a sense they have earned their closeness to nature through a sensitive and devout observation of rituals—hunting codes, annual pilgrimages to hunting sites, and so on. The meaning of ritual as a way of dealing with the Other (including the wilderness) is explored more fully in chapter 4.[29] For now it is enough to note that the relationship with nature that is assumed to be intrinsic to women is maintained by men only through a constant reaffirmation of their respective boundaries and of the rules of the relationship itself—exactly what ritual accomplishes.

For Joe, who can never achieve wholeness because his dual nature is the central fact of his existence, the defense against threats to his sense of self is to avoid adding to the confusion about what is part of him and what is not. He tries not to eat and, thus, not to have to assimilate anything new, to keep himself clean and avoid dirt (= earth = woman), to pay for all he takes, and so on. But the fact that his body remains fundamentally alien to him is reflected in the detachment he seems to experience whenever he is attacked. He watches his own pain as if from a distance:[30] "Lying peaceful and still Joe watched the stranger lean down and lift his head from the floor and strike him again in the face, this time with a short slashing blow. After a moment he licked his lip a little, somewhat as a child might lick a cooking spoon. He watched the stranger's hand go back. But it did not fall" (LA 205). Joe's body becomes a palpable obstacle—"it"—as he tries to leave: "*If I can just get it outside, into the air, the cool air, the cool dark.* He watched his hands fumbling at the door, trying to help them, to coax and control them. 'Anyway, they didn't lock it on me,' he thought. . . . 'It never would have opened a window and climbed through it'" (LA 210).

Significantly, Faulkner as omniscient narrator contributes to this detachment by rhetorically isolating inner aspects of Joe as if they act apart from his conscious self: "He was not thinking at all, not suffering. Perhaps he was conscious of somewhere within him the two severed wireends of volition and sentience lying, not touching now, waiting to touch, to knit anew so that he could move" (LA 207). Notice the bewildering "perhaps" as the narrator implies that whether or not Joe is aware of them, his volition and his sentience are "waiting" to "touch." Faulkner's narrators will frequently reify an abstraction in this manner. More importantly, here is an instance in which a character's perceptions and Faulkner's narrative technique reflect the same dynamic. Faulkner controls Joe's important motivations (and to some extent those of Hightower, Percy Grimm, and Lucas Burch/"Brown") by isolating and reifying his thought processes into external necessities that move him. In this way magical thinking is created in the language of the novel to represent the dissociation in a character's mind between himself and his actions. For Percy Grimm, there is literally a Player who intervenes to determine where he is to be and when during his pursuit of Joe Christmas. Not Grimm's vengeance, but the Player's, destroys Joe (LA 437–439). And Lucas Burch, trying to get his reward and escape from Lena, feels himself being "moved here and there by an Opponent who could read his moves before he made them and who created spontaneous rules which he and not the Opponent, must follow" (LA 414).

Similarly, Faulkner often accelerates either the actions or the perceptions of his characters to disconnect them: "thought was going too fast to give him time to think" (LA 377). He employs speeded up or slow-motion action, time-bound (compulsive use of watches, feeling constrained by time, etc.) versus timeless events, and deliberate confusions and flashbacks in time to suggest both the intensity of subjective experience and a separation of feeling from event—a distancing. Faulkner is just as concerned with boundaries in temporal matters as he is in describing situations or personalities. Splitting serves the function for him of isolating the "otherness" of life through a pretense of separateness: for white males, the female and the black; for crucial events, their affects; for the present moment, the past. The number of Faulknerian characters motivated or isolated solely because of an obsession with some ancestral event implies a message from Faulkner: that the South itself needs to distinguish its present identity from the more appealing myths of the past, which are no longer viable. The blurring of temporal boundaries leads to decay and disintegration, a condition we will see reflected visibly in the personalities of Gail Hightower and Joanna Burden.

Faulkner's technique of splitting characters into different aspects (sentient, volitional, perceiving) or positing a Player in a chess game moving the characters as if they have no will of their own is similar in effect to the conceptual splitting of the male from the female/black that we have already seen contributing to the affective intensity of the novel. Splitting creates distances between things and asserts that there are differences between them by naming the boundaries that locate those differences; thus, volition is both opposed and juxtaposed to sentience, blackness to whiteness. Splitting, moreover, handles ambivalence effectively because it externalizes troublesome entities and denies the interrelatedness of things in a world of flux. Consequently, even Joe's need for a sense of identity can be seen as a wish to impose boundaries (definition, stability) on something which, for him, seems to flow among more or less insubstantial states.[31]

Our reading of Faulkner's prose is an experience which oscillates between flowing with his words and sentence rhythms and trying to keep track of facts and plot to find our place, as it were, by locating those tangible things—facts, names, dates—that serve as points of reference preventing chaos. Faulkner loves to confuse us. He often gives the same name to a grandfather and a grandchild (or uncle and niece, as with Quentin in *The Sound and the Fury*), skipping generations but repeating the same names several times, so that experiences become fused and confused in our minds. Yet he provides appendices, chronologies, genealogies, and maps of Yoknapatawpha County to assure us (and perhaps himself) that everything does indeed have its place, its boundary. Much of the appeal of Faulkner's prose, it seems to me, comes from its powerfully rhythmic effect. It is felt in his continual allusions to dualities and polarities such as those I have already pointed out but also through the rhythms that lead from moments when such distinctions are emphasized to the times when they relax and events and emotions are allowed to flow together, and then back to being separate again. Even within single sentences, Faulkner rhythmically and, therefore, with control leads us through experiences that tend of their own accord to flow together.

The chess game metaphor (cf. the title *Knight's Gambit*) is especially appropriate to Faulkner's perceptual style, because the movements from the black square to the white square are movements between two possibilities, a crossing of lines which themselves remain firm and clear. Through the game metaphor and in other ways (see chapter 3), Faulkner can *play* with the idea of crossing lines,[32] while the terms in which he sets things up, like the chessboard itself, insist that the distinctions are still valid. His preoccupation with boundaries is also a preoccupation with their loss, collapse, or blurring.

Rather often—especially in the flashbacks to crucial moments in Joe's past when his sense of himself was being ingrained by the fanatical Doc Hines and the inflexible Calvinist Simon McEachern—the reader of *Light in August* confronts sentences like these: "Memory believes before knowing remembers. Believes longer than recollects, longer than knowing even wonders. Knows remembers believes a corridor in a big long garbled cold echoing building . . . orphans in identical and uniform blue denim in and out of remembering but in knowing constant as the bleak walls" (LA 111). "Thinking" and "memory" become the subjects of sentences in Faulkner's careful epistemology, which defines the different types of cognition in terms of whether or not a character is currently and actively aware of them. Thus, Joe "knows" and acts upon personal experience that he is not in any sense conscious of, that is not available in his memory of potential ("preconscious") thoughts. What has happened to him is part of his "essence" if not his memory and is "known" in the sense that he cannot act apart from it. The reader is provided with the sum of his knowledge, with a lot more than Joe can recall of his own memories and motivations. In this way Faulkner presents the irrational and the unthought—essential elements of Joe's personality. He manages to give the effect of a psychic determinism that at the same time defends Joe from a direct confrontation with his dichotomous position or its sources: "he had forgotten [the fact of menstruation], in the sense that a fact is forgotten when it once succumbs to the mind's insistence that it be neither true nor false" (LA 174). Faulkner's technique here—again, a type of conceptual splitting—underlines the distinction between the fundamental elements of Joe's personality and Joe's sense of identity (conscious self-awareness, self-image) as he reveals to the reader the developmental sources for Joe's feelings of drivenness and predetermination: "he believed with calm paradox that he was the volitionless servant of the fatality in which he believed that he did not believe. He was saying to himself *I had to do it* already in the past tense; *I had to do it. She said so herself*" (LA 264). These are Joe's thoughts—*before* he murders Joanna.

The feeling of being determined and, by extension, the belief in predestination are virtually unavoidable when personalities are described as if parts of themselves are unknowable and have their own volition.[33] Faulkner's stories suggest a belief in determinism as much because of his narrative style as through any philosophic conviction. It is inherent in his modes of perception that aspects of a single personality are seen as acting apart from one another. Faulkner's habit of splitting things into ever smaller components has the effect of avoiding a need to describe the inconsistencies and complexities of a single personality or situation. By saying that one thing is really two—one of Faulkner's most striking narrative characteristics—he can pretend a cohesiveness that is not felt, a duality in unity. An important example of this is Faulkner's insistence that we always be aware of the dissociation between what a character does and how he feels about it. Emotions are the most intense form of reality in his world. The nuances of feelings are often only contiguously associated with events. *Absalom, Absalom!* is about events and facts that are never verified, and the apparent anxiety of dealing so fully with feelings, impressions, and surmises is balanced and perhaps ameliorated by the pages of documentation (chronology, genealogy, map) that Faulkner attached to the end of this novel. Interestingly, he refused to write an appendix to *The Sound and the Fury* that would be factually consistent with the original novel, written fifteen years earlier. Instead, he wrote an appendix in terms of its emotional truth for him, not even rereading the novel. As he phrased it, "I dont want to read TSAF again. Would rather let the appendix stand with inconsistencies . . . The inconsistencies in the appendix prove that to me the book is still alive after 15 years, and being alive is still growing, changing" and "I dont care much for facts, am not much interested in them, you cant stand a fact up, you've got to prop it up, and when you move to one side a little and look at it from that angle, it's not thick enough to cast a shadow in that direction."[34] Facts, then, not terribly important in their own right, serve in Faulkner's prose as points of reference around which the real life of a novel can move, as boundaries tenuously controlling the flow of experience and emotion.

Descriptions of other characters in *Light in August* reveal additional elements of Faulkner's narrative style, especially his use of the formula "one is two" to structure our experience of those characters. Several of them, like Joe, have manifestly dual natures. Gail Hightower and Joanna Burden are each androgynous figures who move back and forth in the eyes of their acquaintances between their masculine and feminine potentials. As I mentioned earlier, there never seems to be the possibility of integration or wholeness for such figures, and it seems likely that this inner discord would help to explain the degree to which Faulkner's characters are viewed as models of alienation, as stereotypes, or at best as incomplete figures.

Gail Hightower and Joanna Burden are split-off replicas (a feminine male and a manlike female) of one of Faulkner's best-known characters, Emily Grierson in "A Rose for Emily," written a year before *Light in August*. Emily herself is an androgynous figure, both "a slender figure in white" (CS 123) and "a small, fat woman in black" (CS 121), who is described visually in terms of blackness and whiteness throughout her brief story. She has the iron-gray "hair of an active man" (CS 128), yet looks "bloated, like a body long submerged in motionless water" (CS 121). To be bloated or obese-looking or to have a false pregnancy are in Faulkner's stories conditions of decay, the parody and obverse side of creativity, symbolized by having a baby. Lena's fullness of life is reflected in her burgeoning stomach; her healthiness is paralleled by stagnation and decay in the bodies of Emily, Gail, and Joanna. All three are clinging to a past that no longer exists. They have old, unpainted, relatively secluded houses that scarcely anyone visits; their homes, like themselves, smell noticeably. Hightower has a "flabby body" (LA 368) and an "obese stomach like some monstrous pregnancy" (LA 291). Joanna has a false pregnancy and as she clings most tenaciously to Joe, she gets fat. Emily's china-painting lessons, her appearance as an eastern idol (puffy, sedentary, aloof), and her silhouetted figure in windows or door frames all tie her to Joanna and Hightower, who share one or more of these traits. Faulkner depicts decay and stasis, as he does life and creativity, as qualities visible at the surfaces of things. One of the meanings of the title *Light in August* suggests the serenity with which Lena accepts becoming "light" in August, in other words, having her own body's boundaries change radically at her baby's birth yet never feeling that her sense of herself has been jeopardized. Emily, Joanna, and Gail do not have identities firmly rooted either in their true sexuality or in the present moment, in reality; such existential confusions in Faulkner's world always erupt on the surfaces of things.

Throughout Joe's relationship with Joanna, he is incapable of reconciling their nighttime sexual encounters with her daytime, rather sexless appearance in an "apparently endless succession of clean calico house dresses" (LA 220). *"Under her clothes she cant even be made so that it could have happened"* (LA 222). "It was as though there were two people: the one whom he saw now and then by day and looked at while they spoke to one another with speech that told nothing at all since it didn't try to and didn't intend to; the other with whom he lay at night and didn't even see, speak to, at all" (LA 219). Faulkner describes even their emerging sexual relationship in terms of stages which alternate between masculine and feminine modes of being in the world. Joe is able to risk closeness to her at first because of the "hard, untearful and unselfpitying and almost manlike yielding of [her] surrender" (LA 221). "There was no feminine vacillation, no coyness . . . It was as if he struggled physically with another man for an object of no actual value to either . . . she had resisted to the very last . . . resisted fair, *by the rules* that decreed that upon a certain crisis one was defeated, whether the end of resistance had come or not" (LA 222, emphasis mine). And, "she would never stay while he atc" (LA 220). After the second phase begins, Joe feels as if he has "fallen into a sewer" and looks back "As upon another life . . . upon that first hard and manlike surrender . . . as when a defeated general . . . surrenders his sword" (LA 242). Regimentation, the rules of battle, ritual, and Joanna's manlike capitulation had made the relationship one Joe could enjoy. In the second phase, however, Joe has to deal with her urgent, insatiable lust: "Christmas watched her pass through every avatar of a woman in love. Soon she more than shocked him: she astonished and bewildered him" (LA 244). But still, "by day he would see the calm, coldfaced, almost manlike, almost middle-aged woman" (LA 244).

Joe is kept from escaping from Joanna by a type of inertia, a combination of horror and fascination at what she will be capable of next. Like Medusa ("her wild hair . . . like octopus tentacles," LA 245), she immobilizes her man and renders him impotent to leave her. The third and final phase of their affair—the ebbing of their passion, the reproachfulness, and Joanna's movements toward a religious expiation—continues to reveal a sense of dichotomy in Joanna's personality: "what he now saw by daylight was a phantom of someone whom the night sister had murdered and which now moved purposeless about the scenes of old peace, robbed even of the power of lamenting" (LA 248). The elements that Faulkner chooses to set in opposition to one another are not always the same, even within a single characterization such as Joanna's, but he regularly depicts conflict and complexity in major characters in terms such as these, which, by opposing attitudes or qualities, juxtapose them, and by juxtaposing, assert a distinction that guarantees their separateness and difference.

Hightower, too, is a dualistic figure: "His face is at once gaunt and flabby; it is as though there were two faces, one imposed upon the other, looking out from beneath the pale, bald skull. . . . That part of his torso visible above the desk is shapeless, almost monstrous, with a soft and sedentary obesity. He sits rigid" (LA 82). He smells of "plump unwashed flesh . . . that odor of unfastidious sedentation, of static overflesh" (LA 282). Hightower's motionlessness as he waits for his fantasy at twilight and as he listens to Byron's story about Lena suggests both a Buddha-like denial of involvement ("his attitude is that of an eastern idol," LA 83) and a feminine type of stasis—he reads Tennyson. After he involves himself with Lena and with genuine female creativity by helping her to have her child, Hightower can again reach the maleness in himself, so to speak, and he goes home and selects *Henry IV*, "food for a man" (LA 383).

The essence of Hightower's existence is found in his reliving, each evening at dusk, the moment of his grandfather's charge through Jefferson during the Civil War. The war is an event that Faulkner represents as the most courageous, most noble moment in Southern history, albeit a foolish and tragic one, but it is also something in the past that can never be recovered. It is, in a real sense, a refusal to recognize the temporal boundary of the Civil War, to define it as "past," that creates so much confusion for some of Faulkner's protagonists, obsessed by events which they continue to confuse with the present.[35] It is worth noting that even this essential event, which has come to dominate Hightower's thoughts about his own existence, exists in two versions. His grandfather, another Gail Hightower, died in one account when he was shot from a galloping horse in a cavalry charge to defend Jefferson (LA 451); in another, he was shot "likely enough [by] the wife of a Confederate soldier" while stealing chickens from a local henhouse (LA 459).

Faulkner's preoccupation with dualities goes beyond these complex instances of confused sexual identity and is found wherever characters are torn between possibilities. Even Lena Grove, characteristically serene about everything, is described in this way in her thoughts about Lucas Burch: "It's like she was in two parts, and one of them knows that he is a scoundrel. But the other part believes that when a man and a woman are going to have a child, that the Lord will see that they are all together when the right time comes. . . . if the Lord dont see fit to let them two parts meet and kind of compare, then I [Byron] aint going to do it either" (LA 285). Lucas Burch himself has two names, two identities, in order to escape his responsibilities. And minor characters, such as Hightower's father, share in the duality: "he was *two separate and complete people*, one of whom dwelled by serene rules in a world where reality did not exist" (LA 448, emphasis mine). This mode of perception is Faulkner's own, and we encounter it repeatedly in his fiction.[36] The "one is two" formula, the number two in general, and Faulkner's many parallel or dual constructions in his sentences recur so often as to punctuate his thought and contribute to the rhythms of his prose. As I show in a later chapter, Faulkner's love for neologisms ("fecundmellow," "pinkwomansmelling," "manhard") and oxymora ("humbly and with pride") also reflects the dynamic of insisting on the "two-ness" of single objects or situations.

The splitting that generates such dualities implicitly affirms the independence of the parts (which the phrase "two separate and complete people" above emphasizes), as if the parts themselves have their own integrity and identity. Faulkner typically represents this careful separation in strongly visual terms, as he does in the following passage describing Joanna Burden late in her relationship with Joe:

> Anyway, he stayed, watching the two creatures that struggled
> in the one body like two moongleamed shapes struggling
> drowning in alternate throes upon the surface of a black
> thick pool beneath the last moon. Now it would be that still,
> cold, contained figure of the first phase who, even though
> lost and damned, remained somehow impervious and im-

pregnable; then it would be the other, the second one, who
in furious denial of that impregnability strove to drown in
the black abyss of its own creating that physical purity which
had been preserved too long now even to be lost. Now and
then they would come to the black surface, locked like sisters; the black waters would drain away.   (LA 246)

In this remarkable passage Faulkner has polarized the elements of
Joanna's personality into opposites, one asserting and the other denying the very same facts: impregnability, purity (its preservation
and its loss). The elements are "sisters," tangible, struggling, and
self-willed. In dramatic and mythological terms, Faulkner depicts a
struggle made simple conceptually (the pure versus the damned)
because he has so completely bifurcated the elements he opposes.
Again his vision assumes Manichaean dimensions.

   Although his subject matter changed, Faulkner's perceptual
style retained this characteristic throughout his career. He was fascinated, for example, with composite figures, such as the mythical
creatures who were part man and part beast. His first group of
poems was entitled *The Marble Faun* (1924), and he continued to
exploit the pastoral evocativeness of the goat/man image sporadi-
cally for some time. Similarly, in a short story called "Centaur in
Brass," which was later incorporated into *The Town*, the horse/man
figure became a metaphor superimposed on his vision of Flem
Snopes. Hybrid figures played a continuing role in his imagination.
In *The Town* the image is used for comic effect. A young Negro,
Turl, has just flung back the quilt of a bed, expecting to find old
Tom Tom's young wife. Instead, the elderly Tom Tom lies there
with a butcher knife:

   ". . . as on time as two engines switching freight cars. Tom
   Tom must a made his jump jest exactly when Turl whirled to
   run, Turl jumping out of the house into the moonlight again
   with Tom Tom and the butcher knife riding on his back so
   that they looked jest like—what do you call them double-
   jointed half-horse fellers in the old picture books?"
      "Centaur," Gowan said.
   "—looking jest like a centawyer running on its hind legs
   and trying to ketch up with itself with a butcher knife about
   a yard long in one of its extry front hoofs . . ."   (T 26)

With the word "centawyer," of course, Faulkner again plays with the idea of "two in one," splicing together "centaur" and "lawyer" in a comical and characteristic parody of country speech.

It is notable, as well, that precisely as Faulkner evokes the unreal, mythical images of the centaur and faun, he denies their elusiveness with the words "brass" and "marble," which assert that the figures are permanent, tangible, and substantial. Readers familiar with Faulkner will recognize this tendency to focus upon the solidity of objects. His descriptions regularly use analogies to statues, metals, stone, iron filigree, Buddha figures, figures framed by doors and windows, and so on. It is unnecessary to elaborate on this technique of his, which has been thoroughly explored by critics.[37] For our purposes, it is enough to realize that frozen movement and tableau-like descriptions suggest an interest in capturing the essence of a moment or personality by attributing to it the permanence and rigidity of objects of metal, stone, or wood. The outlines of such figures are always visually distinct.[38] Like boundaries, they insist upon the separateness and autonomy of that which they delineate. The narrative emphasis on boundaries and tableaux tends to counteract the insubstantiality, inexpressibility, and flow of experience by declaring quite the opposite: solidity, permanence, and the capacity for definition.

Faulkner's fictive world is a distinctly spatial one, in which the location and movements of characters are important both to the plot and symbolically in terms of the characters' progress through life. The circularity of Joe's travels leads him back to his sources, his fate, when he ends up in the town where, unknown to him, his grandparents live. For Joe, as we have seen, circularity feels like determinism and entrapment; he cannot escape himself, women, or his fate ("I have never got outside that circle . . ."). The theme of wandering or circling may also be seen as reflecting Joe's search for a sense of identity, the return to the same place as the obsessional search for definition, a looking again and again for the same boundary. That the repetitiveness of these movements leaves him feeling trapped is based in the paradox that the feminine/black is experienced simultaneously as "self" and as "other," as security or identity and as entrapment. Lena returns, too, to her fate; she fulfills her identity. But Lena's life returns like thread to a "spool," a source at the end of a finite road, and thus hers is a comfortable homecoming. Her circles/cycles are the feminine ones of menstruation and of birth and the rhythms of eating and sleeping. The novel itself has this circular sense of completion or accomplishment, returning to Lena in the last chapter. Beyond this, rivers, meadows, roads, and woods are suggestive topographical features in the stories since they often carry comparable associations for the characters who move among them.[39]

Faulkner views even time in explicitly spatial terms.[40] He describes the conception of time of the old people in "A Rose for Emily," for example, by saying that the old confuse "time with its mathematical progression . . . to whom all the past is not a diminishing road but, instead, a huge meadow which no winter ever quite touches, divided from them now by the narrow bottle-neck of the most recent decade of years" (CS 129). Spatializing more or less abstract concepts and describing them in markedly visual terms (as drama or map or tableau) are clearly consistent with the technique of isolating and creating borders around entities that we have seen Faulkner use so often. A spatial orientation implicitly assumes that the location and definition of something (the conceptual drawing of a line around it) fixes it somehow. This illusion of control, as Walter Ong and others have suggested,[41] is implicit in the act of writing, which by virtue of its finitude—the words on a page—seems to help us to represent tangibly the entities we are trying to think about. Authors write, in part, to capture their thoughts and feelings by defining them, by giving them dimensions which then feel manageable or manipulable. Faulkner's analogies, metaphors, and similes suggest that such a spatial bias extends throughout his imagination.

However, despite Faulkner's affinity for the visual (the vividness of his descriptions, his dramatic rendering even of cerebral events), there is an important sense in which vision is a way of knowing that fails in his fiction. Too often it is deceptive. Joe Christmas, for example, cannot trust the whiteness of his own skin, which admits the possibility that he may be black; if he were black, he would *know*. When sight fails, distinctions fail, and in Joe's instance, identity is brought into question. Joe's sight also cannot help him to reconcile what he sees of Joanna in the daytime with what he knows of her at night. And Byron Bunch, too, finds that his sight has failed him. He does not really believe that Lena is going to have her baby, *"that she is not a virgin"* (LA 380) until the child is born: "It was like for a week now his eyes had accepted her belly without his mind believing" (LA 377). Faulkner has again chosen to express a perceptual disjunction in terms of a splitting; he depicts Byron's mind and his eyes as separate and contradictory sources of knowledge.

By contrast, the senses of smell and hearing convey infallible truths, even though they are affectively more threatening. Vision involves distance and the ability to locate the boundaries of the other ("he is there"). Smell and sound convey immediacy and in-disputable presence, because they happen within us in intimate conjunction with our internal sensory organs. Consequently, they confirm a presence that may be dangerous ("he is here") and un-controllable. We can close our eyes so as not to see, but we cannot avoid odors or sounds in the same way. The potency of sound is emphasized early in *Light in August* when Lena thinks about hear-ing the wagon long before and long after she can see it. Her fantasy about finding Lucas reflects again the notion of "twos" and "ones" (the "two in one" of pregnancy) as well as a splitting apart of the various modes of knowing: "And if he is going all the way to Jeffer-son, I will be riding within the hearing of Lucas Burch before his seeing. He will hear the wagon, but he wont know. So there will be one within his hearing before his seeing. And then he will see me and he will be excited. And so there will be two within his seeing before his remembering" (LA 6).

While hearing and smell do not necessarily reveal the nature or identity of a presence, as in the quotation above, they do infallibly reveal the *fact* of a presence, as sight can fail to do. The sounds of insects humming pervade many of Faulkner's stories, including *Light in August*, as if to suggest an ongoing presence or a reality that is coextensive with the confusions of events that are merely seen and thought of in the novel's more salient plot. Whereas vision can confuse you, smell and sound forcefully transmit messages of com-fort or alarm. Five-year-old Joe, when Doc Hines takes him from the orphanage, is not surprised or frightened: "It was pitchdark and cold . . . He knew where he was by the smell . . . knew also by smell that the person who carried him was a man" (LA 127). In contrast, years later, looking at a pair of shoes he has swapped with a Negro, Joe's sight leaves him bewildered; the shoes have left a "mark on his ankles the gauge definite and ineradicable of the black tide creeping up his legs, moving from his feet upward as death moves" (LA 321). And again, Byron Bunch tries to avoid the knowledge of Lena's motherhood by riding away on a mule: "'If I can just get past and out of hearing before she hollers again,' he thought. 'If I can just get past before *I have to hear* her again.' . . . Then he heard the child cry. Then he knew" (LA 379, emphasis mine).

Early in Joe Christmas's life, Faulkner says of him: "he was too young yet to escape from the world of women for that brief respite before he escaped back into it to remain until the hour of his death" (LA 113). The recognition that for Faulkner himself, as well as Joe, a movement or change is usually conceived as an escape from a confining situation is important if we are to comprehend the massive degree of drivenness, alienation, and loneliness that so dominates his stories. In his own life, Blotner and Minter tell us, Faulkner came to see his moves to and from Hollywood, Mississippi, New York, and Virginia as consecutive escapes from such feelings of entrapment. Moreover, his passion for horses, cars, and airplanes—which he shared with several of his protagonists—openly expressed his exhilaration at flights from confinement by offering speed, a sense of independence and self-sufficiency (as well as adventure), and distance separating him from claustrophobic commitments. Drinking, too, brought Faulkner a welcome obliviousness to obligations, deadlines, and similar constraining elements in his life. In a moment of exasperation about the multiple family demands on his freedom and energy, Faulkner wrote:

> I have been trying for about ten years to carry a load that no artist has any business attempting: oldest son to widowed mothers and inept brothers and nephews and wives and other female connections and their children, most of whom I dont like and with none of whom I have anything in common . . . if I can just get some money, I can get away for a while—either in service, or out of it. Incidentally, I believe I have discovered the reason inherent in human nature why warfare will never be abolished: it's the only condition under which a man who is not a scoundrel can escape for a while from his female kin. But now the formation of these Waacs and such gives a man to blink.[42]

We have seen that Faulkner's world is presented in distinctly spatial terms and that concepts, personalities, situations, and even the passage of time tend to be spatialized and managed in terms of spatial assumptions. Faulkner splits things apart, draws boundaries around them, insists upon their separateness, and as we will soon see, then plays with the possibility of their reunion or fusion. His strongly visual bias implies the manageability of tangible and locatable objects, while the emotional content of his stories reveals, instead, his characters' anxiety and loneliness in their awareness of continuing change. The quality of their perceptions suggests that only knowledge that places personal boundaries in jeopardy by threatening confusion between the self and other is dependable knowledge. Sound and smell indicate reality powerfully, yet they leave characters feeling out of control. Faulkner's strongly visual descriptions assert the finitude and tangibility of experiences that sound and smell insist, to the contrary, are transient, elusive, or threatening. The paradox at the center of Faulkner's perceptual style is an emotional need for boundaries and certitude to deny the flux that his characters experience both as powerfully real and as jeopardizing their lives or their identities. One's illusion of personal permanence can be sustained only in a world felt to be stable. When Faulkner's characters are forced to be aware of flux and change, certitude is destroyed. Faulkner structures perceptions of the world in ways that allow it subjectively to be a safe and stable place to be. At the same time, he seeks out those media—drink, horses, flying—that allow him to play with the idea of transcending the safe and stable world of boundaries when he feels trapped by it.

In his biography of Faulkner, Joseph Blotner reveals that during the periods when Faulkner's drinking became dangerous, his friends were alerted to his disintegrating control of things by his habit at such times of reciting Shakespeare's "The Phoenix and the Turtle."[43] This poem is remarkable evidence of the fascination that the formula "one is two" held for Faulkner's imagination. The subject of the poem is the love of two mythical creatures for one another, a love that denies their separateness and declares, instead, their unity as a single being. A poem about merger or the collapse of distinctions is especially appropriate for someone immersing himself in drink, since alcohol invites a collapse of claustrophobic restrictions, rules, and expectations. To recite such a poem, in contrast, is to act out the rhythms of control—meter, rhyme, stanza, the memorized words in their given order—simultaneously as one celebrates the oblivion of merger. In other words, recitation is a de-

cidedly structured and controlled way of withdrawing into the inner realms of one's own psyche (through drink) and into the fantasy
of oblivion (through the poem's story).[44]

Stanzas 7, 8, 10, and 11 are worth recalling, for the reader of
Faulkner's prose finds echoes of them throughout his stories:

> So they loved, as love in twain
> Had the essence but in one,
> Two distincts, division none;
> Number there in love was slain.
>
> Hearts remote, yet not asunder;
> Distance, and no space was seen
> 'Twixt this turtle and his queen;
> But in them it were a wonder.
>
> Property was thus appalled,
> That the self was not the same;
> Single nature's double name
> Neither two nor one was called.
>
> Reason, in itself confounded,
> Saw division grow together,
> To themselves yet either neither,
> Simple were so well compounded,[45]

The love of the phoenix and the turtledove destroys their separate identities. It annihilates "selfhood" in the sense of individual
wholeness and independence. Their fusion implies the loss of all
distinctions. They become the same thing, yet "either neither"—
having now no identity and no name. Names and identities are
grounded in differences that make things distinguishable from one
another. The paradox of "distance, and no space," of "hearts remote, yet not asunder" is illogical only from the point of view of
reason; emotionally, it has validity. The dissolution of boundaries
is, after all, a psychic phenomenon asserting the irrelevance of the
concepts "distance," "space," "identity," and "names" and cele-
brating the intensity of emotion. Such a loss of distinctions is Dio-
nysian, a madness and ecstasy classically associated with drink.

Our reading of Faulkner's prose and his writing itself share the
rhythms of control and relaxing into the flow of experience that his
recitation of this poem seems to symbolize. We sometimes feel ourselves on the verge of losing control as we move through his end-

less sentences, repeated flashbacks, and deliberate obfuscations of events. Yet the rhythms of his words themselves, his sentence constructions, his establishment of spatial and temporal boundaries, and the facts that serve as reference points for how events are related to one another help us to link together enough data to know what the story is "about." We play with the pleasure of not quite knowing, because Faulkner always ultimately controls things and shows us where we are. The elusiveness of the subject matter itself, however, suggests that Faulkner contradicts what he is writing about by the act of writing. He writes, in many ways, about the fusion or confusion of events and personalities, yet writing makes them finite, implies their tangibility, and offers the illusion of control. That the act of writing itself felt antithetical to his experience of life we can see in this quotation from *Mosquitoes* in which Faulkner speaks of the writer "with a notebook in his hand always, putting down all the charming things that ever happen to him, *killing them* for the sake of some problematical something he might or he might not ever use" (MOS 320, emphasis mine). With his prose Faulkner attempts both to fix and to preserve the chaotic and elusive experiences that seem to defy description through their intensity and transience: "nothing served but that I try by main strength to recreate between the covers of a book the world as I was already preparing to lose and regret . . . desiring, if not the capture of that world and the feeling of it as you'd preserve a kernel or a leaf to indicate the lost forest, at least to keep the evocative skeleton of the dessicated [sic] leaf." [46]

Chapter Two
Precarious Coherence: Objects through Time

As though the clotting which is you had dissolved into the
myriad original motion   *As I Lay Dying*, p. 156

When we look closely at Faulkner's descriptions of objects and
activities that exist through the course of time, we discover that
his perceptual style continues to rely heavily on the imagistic visu-
alization of his concern with transience. Faulkner is never able to
leave behind his awareness that the life around him is pervaded by
change, and his descriptions visually suggest this preoccupation by
focusing on disintegration taking place at objects' surfaces and
by avoiding direct descriptions of motion in favor of oblique approaches, such as creating "frozen moments" or "tableaux." As he
depicts motion and the existence of objects in time, his prose expresses a continuing awareness of time's ravages.

   As various critics have noted, Faulkner's prose reveals a number of affinities with the thoughts of Henri Bergson on the nature of
reality and our perception of it.[1] Bergson held that whether we believe the fundamental component of life to be mind or matter, our
intuitive understanding forces us to acknowledge that life is characterized by its quality of continuous change, or "becoming." He
calls this perpetual becoming "flux"; it involves life's ongoing
emergence into potentials that are never fully realized, since that
would be the end of change and, hence, death. Flux is the essential
feature both of physical substances (or objects) and of mental processes. One cannot be the same person on two separate occasions,
for example, because we cannot live the same moment twice. Our
existence through time involves a perpetual accumulation of experiences, each of which alters the sum of our previous experiences.
It is evident, in this view, that we can never return to any moment
in the past, for intervening moments have irrevocably altered us.

   This accretion of events—the omnipresence of the past in the
evolving present—gives to our experience of time a quality that
Bergson calls "durée" or "duration." Although it is not possible to
verify the source for Faulkner's use of the term, we cannot help but

think of his famous synopsis of the lives of such figures as Dilsey, found in his 1945 Appendix to *The Sound and the Fury*: "They endured" (TSAF 427).[2] For Faulkner, endurance involves precisely an awareness of the multifariousness of accumulating experience and of the fullness of life. There are significant differences between this type of existence, which connotes serenity and an acceptance of things as they are, and the simple tenacity evinced by those Faulknerian characters who live in the past. Their lives are effectively over, as Faulkner reminds us repeatedly in imagery of deadness and stagnation. We have seen this already in the figures of Emily Grierson, Joanna Burden, and Gail Hightower, whose antipathy to life is vividly suggested in false pregnancies and similar grotesqueries. To accept the present moment with its myriad implications is to grow with it and change because of it. The rigidity of not being able to do so is the source of much anguish for Faulkner's time-entrapped characters.

In spite of our intuition's recognition of the fluidity of experience, Bergson argued, our rational faculty is able to contemplate the realities presented to it only by assuming a stability that contradicts our subjective experience of flux and duration. Immanuel Kant had recognized this characteristic of the rational mind when he asserted that "space" and "time" are forms of perception which organize a priori the experience of all phenomena. We are incapable of thinking of anything without spatializing it—which intrinsically assumes a degree of finitude and stability—or temporalizing it in a manner that assumes linearity and succession and, again, finitude. As Bergson describes it:

> preoccupied before everything with the necessities of action, the intellect, like the senses, is limited to taking, at intervals, views that are instantaneous and by that very fact immobile of the becoming of matter. . . . Of becoming we perceive only states, of duration only instants, and even when we speak of duration and of becoming, it is of another thing that we are thinking. Such is the most striking of the two illusions we wish to examine. It consists in supposing that we can think the unstable by means of the stable, the moving by means of the immobile.[3]

This is the paradox that underlies Faulkner's apparently self-contradictory manner of depicting motion and change. On the one hand, he continually tries to come to terms with and describe the flux of experience, including its subjective urgency, its elusiveness, and its ephemerality. On the other, while he is doing so, his prose expresses a need to control described objects, especially affectively potent ones, by spatializing them: seeing them in strongly visual terms, splitting them apart, focusing on the boundaries that separate and define them as distinct from one another, and so on. The rhythm of flowing and control that I explicate throughout this book is a rhythm created by his relative stressing of (1) the flux of experience as it tends to flow with its own momentum and (2) the illusion of stability implicit in asserting the finitude or boundedness of objects in this same reality.

On occasions when Faulkner and Bergson attempt to describe the subjective experience of continuity through time and change, they have chosen remarkably similar imagery. Describing the passage of time, Faulkner frequently imagines roads, tunnels, and corridors, which appear to close behind us and open at our approach, as time does. In a similar way, Bergson has chosen to discuss his own "mental state, as it advances on the road of time . . . continually swelling with the duration which it accumulates."[4] Each of them has chosen a finite, visual representation to suggest the distinction between the *apparent* linearity and succession of time and the subjectively *experienced* fullness of the moments in which we exist.

One of Faulkner's omnipresent images is that of a moving object, often explicitly likened to a bead, on a wire or string. As we have seen, in the first chapter of *Light in August*, Lena Grove perceives a wagon in such terms as it moves through time and space, both as it approaches her on the road and as she later rides on it. The wagon is alternately described as a "shabby bead" and as a "spool" onto which the "mild red string of road" is being rewound (LA 6). Compare this with Bergson as he writes about the illusory nature of states of being, in this instance, the "mental states" of the "ego": "Instead of a flux of fleeting shades merging into each other, [our reason] perceives distinct and, so to speak, *solid* colors, set side by side like the beads of a necklace; it must perforce then suppose a thread, also itself solid, to hold the beads together."[5] Bergson compares our perception of the relationship between states of mind and the ego—and implicitly between any "states" of being and the concept which subsumes them—with that of beads on a thread. He tells us that the distinct entities that reason sees when it focuses on outer reality, as well as the continuity that we posit as we try to comprehend that reality, are illusory. Such *merely apparent* relationships are belied by the radical flux of experience. Faulkner, of course, has used the same imagery to describe the same circumstance—a character's perception of apparent continuity as she waits through time for the arrival and observes the progress of a wagon.

Faulkner habitually uses such images as spools, beads, and tunnels when he tries to assert the stability or sameness of people or objects that move through time and space. This technique is especially evident in Quentin's monologue in *The Sound and the Fury*. As we shall see later in this chapter, Quentin's obsessive need to control his perceptions, because it gives him the illusion of controlling reality, results in a variety of idiosyncratic imaginings, among them his recurrent perception of such figures as birds being suspended between the branches of trees (or the sails of ships) on wires or being dragged by wires through space. This narrative technique and similar ones—in which notably visual images anchor and spatialize (even geometrize) what Faulkner is describing—help Faulkner to bypass the direct description of such phenomena as motion or change by "freezing" the event being described (the flight of birds) into a seemingly stable visual configuration in which everything is "connected" to everything else. An effect of such metaphorical language—intrinsically indirect—is that his descriptions seem to retain the elusiveness of experience. By displacing motion and change themselves onto metaphors, Faulkner acts out the inherent resistance of experience to direct description. He avoids "killing" what he describes (MOS 320) by doing so obliquely.[6]

To describe an object existing through time, Faulkner is forced to deal with the differences that characterize an object from one moment to another. He is conscious both of the transience and intangibility of mere qualities and of the inexpressibility of essences, those fundamental characteristics that allow each of us to remain somehow recognizable as ourselves. In the previous chapter I showed how Faulkner habitually controls objects in proximity to one another, that is to say, how he confronts the problem of describing differences between objects coexisting in space. The differences within a single object from one moment to the next are the temporal equivalent of that descriptive problem. In both instances,

Faulkner focuses his energies on a consideration of the surfaces or edges of things. Just as he emphasized boundaries to assert one object's distinctness from other objects, he also uses them in ways that allow an inference of change or flux within a single object. In other words, he uses boundaries paradoxically, both to emphasize an object's autonomy and separateness and to reveal its fluidity and the precariousness of its identity. This should remind us of the developmental task I outlined in the Introduction: the need to establish a sense of self separate from other objects in the world and yet be able to interact meaningfully with that world (go beyond one's felt boundaries) without feeling that one's identity is being lost, the need to be both separate from and connected to others.

Objects in Faulkner's fictive world tend to display at their surfaces an aura, a penumbra, an emanation—where they are not quite fully themselves but are evolving into something different that they have not quite yet become. Like the rays of the sun in *The Sound and the Fury*, they begin to assume new identities: "Sunlight slanted into it, sparse and eager. Yellow butterflies flickered along the shade like flecks of sun" (TSAF 151); "Sunlight . . . glinting along the pole like yellow ants" (152); "pencils of sun slanted in the trees" (167); "Little flecks of sunlight brushing across my face like yellow leaves" (201); "There was another yellow butterfly, like one of the sunflecks had come loose" (175).

As Faulkner tries narratively to capture the wholeness or essence of an object, it often fragments at its surface into fleeting, less tangible pieces. Many of his most intense descriptive passages are characterized by a recurrence of this elusiveness on the part of the object being described and by a failure of vision to control the perception by making boundaries cohere. In the following excerpt from an interior monologue in *As I Lay Dying*, the child Vardaman confronts his brother's horse:

> It is as though the dark were resolving him out of his integrity, into an unrelated scattering of components—snuffings and stampings; smells of cooling flesh and ammoniac hair; an illusion of a co-ordinated whole of splotched hide and strong bones within which, detached and secret and familiar, an *is* different from my *is*. I see him dissolve—legs, a rolling eye, a gaudy splotching like cold flames—and float upon the dark in fading solution; all one yet neither; all either yet none. I

can see hearing coil toward him, caressing, shaping his hard
shape—fetlock, hip, shoulder and head; smell and sound. I
am not afraid.   (AILD 55)

This passage reflects several of the perceptual habits typical of
Faulkner's characters. Vardaman's recognition of "an *is* different
from my *is*" affirms the importance to him of establishing the
border between self and other. The passage also expresses an intense awareness of the radical flux of matter. Most obvious is the
fragmentation of the horse into discrete elements and of the boy's
perceptions into apparently irreconcilable messages from his various senses. The words "resolving," "illusion," "dissolve," "float,"
and "fading" all appear to describe a type of motion or change. In
fact, however, they only confirm a failure of vision to locate and
sustain the "otherness" of the perceived object, a failure that is
common in Faulkner's world. Sight does not reliably confirm that a
safe distance exists between Vardaman and the horse; instead, it
precipitates the fusion/confusion of "all one yet neither; all either
yet none," a phrase reminiscent of the concerns and the language of
Shakespeare's "The Phoenix and the Turtle." For Vardaman, hearing and smell combine finally to pull together his experience of the
horse by "shaping his hard shape" and locating the tangible "otherness" of the animal.

It is not simply coincidence that Faulkner's techniques for describing motion are especially evident when he writes about horses.
For him horses are the perfect image of sheer masculine energy,
passion, and freedom. Faulkner has Jack Houston (in *The Hamlet*)
buy a stallion at the time of his marriage, and the narrator suggests
that it "represented that polygamous and bitless masculinity which
he had relinquished" (H 214). Wives and stallions represent antithetical states of being; they are natural enemies, irreconcilable,
and soon afterward, "the stallion killed her" (H 215). Only young
boys (Vardaman in *As I Lay Dying* and Wallstreet Snopes in "Spotted Horses") confront wild horses with impunity. Their special immunity, moreover, is clearly associated with their freedom from entanglements with women. The period during which males enjoy this
special freedom is a very short one, as we see in this description of
the still-dependent, five-year-old Joe Christmas: "he was too young
yet to escape from the world of women for that brief respite before
he escaped back into it to remain until the hour of his death"

(LA 113). Dependence, sexuality, and responsibility combine to define most of a man's life in terms of his relationships with women. Freedom is the perquisite of the preadolescent. During a stampede in a corral, Wallstreet Snopes's special kind of immunity, amounting almost to a state of grace, becomes evident:

> he looked behind him and saw the little boy still leaning to the knot-hole in the door which in the next instant vanished into matchwood, the knot-hole itself exploding from his eye and leaving him, motionless in the diminutive overalls and still leaning forward a little until he vanished utterly beneath the towering parti-colored wave full of feet and glaring eyes and wild teeth which, overtopping, burst into scattering units, revealing at last the gaping orifice and the little boy still standing in it, unscathed, his eye still leaned to the vanished knot-hole.   (H 283)

The child-like fascination with horses of Faulkner's male characters reflects a longing for that lost "brief respite" of freedom. Faulkner treats the men who try to capture the wild ponies in "Spotted Horses" comically. To "capture" freedom, to confine it, is a contradiction in terms, and the attempt leads to chaos and destruction. Male characters continually chase horses, fly planes, and drive cars recklessly in their search for irretrievable personal freedom. Wallstreet makes no attempt to control the horses; he is simply with them, a part of what they represent. Not yet unfree, he exists in a purified state of being—in a space ("gaping orifice") that represents a time he will soon leave behind. It is characteristic, then, that horses should be depicted as being out of control and elusive. Visually, they never quite cohere. Even the Compsons' placid family horse manifests the typically fragmented appearance: "Fancy watched me across the fence blotchy like a quilt on a line" (TSAF 186).

Despite the almost frenetic change implied in such descriptions as these by virtue of language that suggests visual confusion at the surfaces of objects, it is somewhat remarkable that Faulkner rarely attempts to describe actual motion and change in themselves. Instead of focusing directly on motion and using the expected active verbs to describe it, he often approaches the narrative problem obliquely. For example, he will tend to describe a rapid succession of visual images that imply the motion necessary to get from one to another, his famous technique of using "frozen mo-

ments." In the following quotation from *As I Lay Dying*, Jewel
wrestles with his horse:

> Save for Jewel's legs they are like two figures carved for a
> tableau savage in the sun.
>   When Jewel can almost touch him, the horse stands on his
> hind legs and slashes down at Jewel. Then Jewel is enclosed
> by a glittering maze of hooves as by an illusion of wings;
> among them, beneath the upreared chest, he moves with the
> flashing limberness of a snake. For an instant before the jerk
> comes onto his arms he sees his whole body earth-free, hori-
> zontal, whipping snake-limber, until he finds the horse's
> nostrils and touches earth again. Then they are rigid, motion-
> less, terrific, the horse back-thrust on stiffened, quivering
> legs, with lowered head; Jewel with dug heels, shutting off
> the horse's wind with one hand, with the other patting the
> horse's neck in short strokes myriad and caressing, cursing
> the horse with obscene ferocity.
>   They stand in rigid terrific hiatus, the horse trembling and
> groaning. Then Jewel is on the horse's back.   (AILD 12)

The descriptive strategy here is the creation of a series of framed
images or tableaux that seem to segment the motion into manageable visual configurations. Bergson calls the tendency of human
consciousness to perceive movement in this way the "cinemato-
graphical mechanism of thought"[7] because it evokes the illusion of
motion in the rapidity with which still scenes are projected on a
motion picture screen. Faulkner achieves this illusion that we are
seeing a series of snapshots by regularly using the word "is" to imply that what he is describing are states of being ("Then Jewel
is . . .," "Then they are . . .") and by emphasizing words like
"hiatus" and "motionless." Although Faulkner obviously uses active verbs as well, it is characteristic of him to turn to copulative
verbs to slow down such "instants" when violence or passion pervades a particular scene.
   Such words as "carved," "tableau," "rigid," and "motionless," moreover, create tension in the passage by their contradiction
of the evanescence suggested by "glittering," "illusion," and "flash-
ing." This tension is evidence of the paradox inherent in Faulkner's
modes of perception. Always we find an impulse to see objects as
stable and finite balanced with an awareness of the dynamic alive-

ness and change that are their essence. A consequence of his dual perspective is Faulkner's indirect approach to descriptions: he tends to focus upon stasis (as in the passage above) to suggest motion while in his descriptions of static objects he stresses their ephemerality. He makes motion an inference that exists among instants described as if *they* exist, but they do not (as Bergson affirmed), and he is fully aware of it. When he describes instants *as* instants, for example, he does so precisely in terms of their deadness. Gail Hightower says of himself in *Light in August*: "for fifty years I have not even been clay: I have been a single instant of darkness in which a horse galloped and a gun crashed . . . I am my dead grandfather on the instant of his death" (LA 465). The moment something is definable (*definire*, "to limit, end"), it is finite and thus, in Faulkner's view, dead: "out of his subconscious [Hightower] produces without volition the few crystallizations of stated instances by which his dead life in the actual world had been governed and ordered once" (LA 346).

This obliquity in Faulkner's approach to what he describes becomes clearer if we look briefly at the concept of figure-ground reversal. An awareness of this perceptual phenomenon is often enlightening in a consideration of Faulkner's modes of perception. In differentiating figure and ground relationships (especially in two-dimensional entities such as pictures, ink-blot drawings, and visual puzzles), the boundary separating and joining the two is crucial to the description of either thing. In the picture in which two faces in profile facing one another become, in an alternate view, a vase, the same boundary defines both entities. If we could somehow precisely delineate the field, we would implicitly also have defined (by locating the exact boundary of) the object. The boundary of one *is* the boundary of the other. In many respects, Faulkner's writing suggests figure-ground reversal techniques. That little perceptual shift that we make in order to see first one thing and then another as the object of such a drawing clarifies our understanding of Faulkner's habitual shifting between the dimension of substantiality of an object and the dimension of its transience. He often turns to the *less important* thing (the field or ground) of the two possible focuses because the obliquity of such a description allows the important thing (the object, whichever thing he wants to preserve) to retain its vitality. The object is thus experientially potent for the reader because it is never limited by the inherent finitude of direct descrip-

Danish psychologist Edgar Rubin first published images illustrating the concept of figure-ground reversal in *Synsoplevede Figurer*, 1915. Here is his best-known illustration, the ambiguous "Peter-Paul Goblet."

tion. It is evoked instead. "Instants" or "states" are described to imply motion and change, yet Faulkner reveals the falsity of these same instants and states, which he never loses sight of, by stressing fragmentation and dissolution in his descriptions of them. In other words, when he tries to isolate an object in time, the illusion that it retains a stable identity (that it remains in a given "state") is consistently undermined by the *appearance* of motion or change conveyed by language that suggests disintegration or turbulence.

A second way in which Faulkner describes motion obliquely rather than directly is to use metaphorical language that compares it with *other* motion. This device has the same effect as the creation of tableaux; it obviates the necessity of using active verbs and of narratively depicting the continuity of action in itself. Perhaps his intention is to avoid describing as if it were objectively real what Faulkner (with Bergson) believes to be essentially an illusion, the notion of continuity. Faulkner's description of Cash as he works on his mother's coffin (AILD 71–75) is one of his infrequent attempts to show motion sustained over a long period of time. It contains no fewer than twenty-two similes about the changing appearance of the coffin and the progress of Cash's labors: "as though he were lifting and dropping them at the bottom of an invisible well," "as if any movement might dislodge them," "as upon a wall," "as though quick with young," "as though of relief," "as though fired from a gun," "as though from beyond time," "as though he had been abruptly turned wrongside out," "as a piston moves in the oil," "slow as cold glycerin," and so on. Using such stylistic techniques,

Faulkner perpetually reminds us of his apparent discomfort at characterizing motion and change directly. The essential feature of life, they elude the finitude of words that could only approximate their nature. Faulkner much prefers *evoking* the quality of the motion he is trying to depict by likening it to the quality of motion in other activities that we presumably will recognize. Not surprisingly, many of his similes create vivid, visual examples of *ways* of being in motion; they have the benefit of not reducing the activity he is talking about to a declarative statement that might not continue to be imaginatively provocative for his readers when they have finished the passage. His similes stay with us; we recall the quality of Cash's work long after we have forgotten the sequence or particulars of it. The evocation has been compelling.

Faulkner's idiosyncratic obliquity in portraying motion has the effect of emphasizing its intensity and contributes to the subjective tension we feel reading his prose as we wait for things to happen or stop happening. Even when he describes static objects, however, he transmits the inexorability of change in ways that make us constantly aware of the effects of time and in ways that keep us, too, somewhat tense with expectation. His conception of the substantiality of physical objects involves the notion that matter is composed of elements which of their own accord would tend to flow into less definable states. Objects are precipitates, distillations, or accretions of matter that coheres only more or less temporarily in Faulkner's universe. In fact, he rarely fails to see the essence even of situations and personalities in terms of a concentration of qualities, ostensibly more definable and denser than what surrounds them, as we saw in the "crystallizations" of moments that defined Hightower's existence.

The sense that simple cohesiveness undergirds the material world is strengthened by Faulkner's many implications that the primordial basic elements constitute objects and humans alike. Proximity to earth and water, for example, seems to coax a significant number of objects in his fictive world into dissolving or losing their boundedness in an apparent regression to a simpler, more nearly anonymous state: "When you leave a leaf in water a long time after awhile the tissue will be gone and the delicate fibers waving slow as the motion of sleep" (TSAF 144); "I lay down on the bank with my face close to the ground so I couldnt smell the honeysuckle I couldnt smell it then and I lay there feeling the earth going through my clothes" (TSAF 193–194);[8] and "Jewel and Vernon are in the river again. From here they do not appear to violate the surface at all; it is as though it had severed them both at a single blow, the two torsos moving with infinitesimal and ludicrous care upon the surface. . . . As though the clotting which is you had dissolved into the myriad original motion . . ." (AILD 156).

The formation of objects is a reversal of this same nebulous process: "The air smells like sulphur. Upon the impalpable plane of it their shadows form as upon a wall, as though like sound they had not gone very far away in falling but had merely congealed for a moment, immediate and musing" (AILD 72). Shadows partake of that twilight world between the subject (self) and the other. In Quentin's section of *The Sound and the Fury*, shadows and the processes of cohesion and dissolution are aggravated by Quentin's own obsession with the effects of the passage of time. His perceptions reveal a preoccupation with the same transience that Faulkner as a writer is never quite at peace with. In one characteristic scene, Quentin tries to wipe off a loaf of bread the little Italian girl is carrying after it has been splashed with water; it disintegrates before his eyes: "I took my handkerchief and tried to wipe the loaf, but the crust began to come off, so I stopped. . . . It looked kind of like rats had been eating it now" (TSAF 172). Even objects quietly existing in time perpetually undergo the processes of fragmentation or dissolution. The neat, serious lady standing behind the bakery counter in this same episode "looked like a librarian. Something among dusty shelves of ordered certitudes long divorced from reality, *desiccating peacefully* . . ." (TSAF 155, emphasis mine).

Three of Faulkner's works are especially useful in a discussion of his habitual ways of dealing with change or motion in objects. "Dry September," *As I Lay Dying*, and Quentin's section of *The Sound and the Fury* are each concerned in fundamental ways with the most radical of changes, that from life to death. Stylistically these stories are characterized by a large number of allusions to inanimate entities (metals, wood, etc.) as opposed to animate ones, as well as by that same tension between the subjective awareness of the flow of experience and the rigidity of particular perceptions that we saw in the last chapter in the descriptions of individuals framed by doorways or silhouetted against backgrounds as if they are especially tangible and permanent: "For an instant longer [Jewel] runs silver in the moonlight, then he springs out like a flat figure cut leanly from tin against an abrupt and soundless explosion as the whole loft of the barn takes fire at once . . ." (AILD 208); "[Jewel] is struggling with Gillespie . . . They are like two figures in a Greek frieze, isolated out of all reality by the red glare" (AILD 211). In such passages the emphasis on the boundaries of the persons involved is not only conveyed by the imagery of rigidity ("cut leanly from tin," "Greek frieze") but also by the fact that these figures are explicitly set against their backgrounds (in these particular cases, moonlight and fire) so that they seem silhouettes whose boundaries are all-important.[9] This dual, figure-ground gestalt recurs in Faulkner's prose, especially at moments of violence.

In these three stories, Faulkner pervasively employs dust, sawdust, earth, wood, sweat, blood, shadows, and such as motifs that focus the changes occurring within objects on their surfaces and enable confusions about life and death themselves to be reflected in confused perceptions. In *As I Lay Dying*, for example, the members of the Bundren family try to come to terms with their feelings about their dead mother and the decaying corpse that has become her only trace. That the moment of death is not a sharp and tangible boundary is reflected in the animate/inanimate duality[10] that Faulkner uses to reinforce their perceptual confusions. Thus, in this story Vardaman's fish "bleeds quietly in the pan" (AILD 57), Addie while still alive "is no more than a bundle of rotten sticks" (43), Jewel's eyes "look like pieces of burnt-out cinder" (30–31), and Cash's arms "look like sand" (57) from working on "the bleeding plank" (62).

Language of metamorphosis suggesting the implications of such perceptions pervades the narratives. In the five sections of the short story "Dry September," Faulkner alternately chooses a vocabulary asserting the violence of the transition from life to death, on the one hand, and (in sections two and four) the illusion of merely apparent life, on the other. The interplay of the parallel stories of Will Mayes and Minnie Cooper largely emerges as a tension created between the distortions of "life" revealed, as always in Faulkner's prose, by the surfaces of things.

The portions of the story dealing with Will Mayes's murder and the passionate hatred leading up to it are saturated with references to the atmosphere (dry, rainless, dusty, suffocating) and to sweating, blood, intense smells, choking, and ubiquitous dust. The "dust unto dust" imagery of the Bible that reminds us of our ultimate mortality and the vanity of those distinctions that seem so important to us in life serves a similar function here by counterpointing the prejudice, hypocrisy, and violence—all based on the illusion of distinctions, of boundaries—that make up the story. Dust infiltrates everything alike as visual testimony to the irrevocability of change and the anonymity to which we all return. This atmosphere, breathed in, creates a confusion of personal boundaries (choking, not being able to catch one's breath) and accelerates the dissolution of objects' surfaces (bleeding, sweating, McLendon's saturated shirt); the distortions of passion merely exacerbate boundary confusion, as we see both visually and in the behavior of the mob that annihilates the individual will. Will Mayes's death itself is framed and symbolized by allusions to a radical absence of air, of sound, and even of sweat, which normally suggest the presence of life, and by the displacement of lifelike motion onto inanimate objects: "Below the east the wan hemorrhage of the moon increased. It heaved above the ridge, silvering the air, the dust, so that they seemed to breathe, live, in a bowl of molten lead. There was no sound of nightbird nor insect, no sound save their breathing and a faint ticking of contracting metal about the cars. Where their bodies touched one another they seemed to sweat dryly, for no more moisture came. 'Christ!' a voice said; 'let's get out of here'" (CS 177); "They went on; the dust swallowed them; the glare and the sound died away. The dust of them hung for a while, but soon the eternal dust absorbed it again" (CS 180).

In contrast, the sections concerning Minnie Cooper[11] reveal rhetorically the artificiality of a life in which change is only apparent. The text here abounds in words that Faulkner uses to signal illusion and falsity. All are visual words: "bright," "mask," "feverish look," "glitter." Minnie's face "began to wear that bright, haggard look . . . like a mask or a flag" (CS 174). Her "bright dresses, her idle and empty days, had a quality of furious unreality" (CS 175). After the "insult," Minnie and her friends attend a picture show whose description reveals how thoroughly she now confuses the dreams reflected on the screen with life. These distorted, romanticized perceptions—implicitly Minnie's—convince us of Mayes's innocence:

They reached the picture show. It was like a miniature fairy-
land . . . they took their accustomed places where she could
see the aisle against the silver glare and the young men and
girls coming in two and two against it.

The lights flicked away; the screen glowed silver, and soon
life began to unfold, beautiful and passionate and sad, while
still the young men and girls entered, scented and sibilant in
the half dark, their paired backs in silhouette delicate and
sleek, their slim, quick bodies awkward, divinely young,
while beyond them the silver dream accumulated, inevitably
on and on.   (CS 181, emphasis mine)

The central event in this story, Mayes's murder, is missing but
is unmistakably indicated. In this sense it is characteristic of a
number of events in Faulkner's stories.[12] Just as importantly, the
event—the insult—that precipitates the action of the story is also
missing, but the text offers innumerable clues that *as* an insult, it
probably never happened. Something that has not happened is the
cause of things that do, all of the events of the story. An absence
generates a presence, including the pseudo-presence of the lynching. As I explain more fully in chapter 3, absences play an important role in justifying and explaining the nature of the things that
are present, thematically and rhetorically, in Faulkner's prose. The
interplay of present and absent things in his fictive world, including central events around which plots are based, is a narrative example of the figure-ground reversal I mentioned earlier. We are told
so much of what leads up to and issues from events—that is, so
much of the background is provided—that we cannot doubt the existence of the missing event. This story, split in two and conducted
along parallel chronological lines, concerns an absent event that
gives the story its only unity. The pattern of splitting things into
two we have seen before; that of positing an absent reality that exists somehow in the interstices between such things is a figure-
ground technique that we will continue to explore.

In *As I Lay Dying* the central event is also missing. It is impossible to locate the moment of Addie's death because Faulkner has
deliberately confused his chronology with multiple interior monologues that overlap, leave gaps, anticipate, and recall events while
the death itself is mentioned only by Darl. He mystically imagines

the events at home surrounding his mother's death, but he is miles away with his brother. Addie's only monologue appears chronologically long after her apparent death; Faulkner seems to emphasize through its placement that her death has been anticipated and becomes a reality for the different people who know her at very different times and for very different reasons. Dr. Peabody is called to Addie's bedside only when it is too late, and as he phrases it, "She has been dead these ten days. . . . I can remember how when I was young I believed death to be a phenomenon of the body; now I know it to be merely a function of the mind—and that of the minds of the ones who suffer the bereavement" (AILD 42). Through Peabody, then, Faulkner defines "death" essentially as a loss—as the presence of an absence in the lives of the bereaved. In a sense the pseudo-presence of Addie, her increasingly offensive corpse, interferes with her family's ability to accept the fact of absence which is death.

The indeterminacy of Addie's death lends irony to the novel's title. It begins to encompass all of the Bundrens, indeed every character in the novel. As critic Roma King has expressed it, "The 'I' may represent . . . all characters, for each is permitted in the novel to express his consciousness, to become the 'I.'" [13] Each character, by virtue of being alive and mortal, is dying, and a few of them are specifically associated with death, deadness, and the inanimate.

Faulkner uses animate-inanimate imagery throughout this novel but with far different effects in different characterizations. Addie's husband, Anse, for example, is seen as dead because of his rigid personality and narrowness of vision. He is one of Faulkner's most exasperating yet comic figures. In Dewey Dell's eyes, Anse "looks like right after the maul hits the steer and it no longer alive and dont yet know that it is dead" (AILD 58). Even Anse's shoes express his personality, looking as if they had been "hacked with a blunt axe out of pig-iron" (AILD 11). But the most salient fact about Anse is that he never sweats: "There is no sweat stain on his shirt. I have never seen a sweat stain on his shirt. He was sick once from working in the sun when he was twenty-two years old, and he tells people that if he ever sweats, he will die. I suppose he believes it" (AILD 16–17). This, of course, is only an excuse that Anse uses never to have to do any work, but his not sweating also suggests his deadness in the sense that he is not changing, evolving as others are, he does not interact genuinely with anyone, and his perceptions are notoriously rigid and self-serving. Unlike characters who work, suffer, and feel passion and whose surfaces uniformly reflect change in life-asserting ways (pregnancy, sweat, tears, bleeding, and so on), Anse merely persists relentlessly in the lives of those who know him.

The distinction is one we are familiar with, staticity and tenacity as opposed to the adaptability and receptivity characteristic of endurance (Bergson's *durèe*). As if to contrast father and son, Faulkner describes Cash in the following terms on the same page on which he compares Anse to a dead steer: "Cash is eating. About his head the print of his hat is sweated into his hair. His shirt is blotched with sweat. He has not washed his hands and arms" (AILD 58).

Empty shoes and other items of clothing in Faulkner's stories are always reflections of the personality they belong to. Characters who leave no trace of themselves on the clothes they wear are notably lifeless in some respect. Flem Snopes in Faulkner's Snopes trilogy leaves no trace of himself just as he leaves no heirs; he is impotent, ruthless, and without humanity.[14] Consequently, when Vernon Tull says of Anse, "I never see him with a shirt on that looked like it was his in all my life" (AILD 30), the description of his physical appearance can be taken as an indication of his personal limitations. Anse is thoroughly narcissistic and self-serving and manages to interpret everything that happens as a deliberate and personal persecution. When his wife becomes sick and he calls the doctor after it is too late to save her, he thinks bitterly, "And now I got to pay for it" (AILD 36); at her death, he expresses only his sense of deprivation. "She taken and left us" (AILD 49). In passages of perfect irony, Anse envisions himself as long-suffering and singled out for torment: "It's a hard country on man; it's hard. Eight miles of the sweat of his body washed up outen the Lord's earth, where the Lord Himself told him to put it. Nowhere in this sinful world can a honest, hardworking man profit. It takes them that runs the stores in the towns, doing no sweating, living off of them that sweats. It aint the hardworking man, the farmer. Sometimes I wonder why we keep at it" (AILD 104).

Jewel, Addie's child by Reverend Whitfield, is repeatedly described through figures of speech suggesting lifelessness: "his pale eyes like wood set into his wooden face, he [walks] . . . with the rigid gravity of a cigar store Indian" (AILD 4); "Jewel's eyes look like marbles" (94); "eyes . . . pale as two bleached chips in his face" (138); "*that bold, surly, high-colored rigid look like his face and eyes were two colors of wood, the wrong one pale and the wrong one dark*" (173); and "his face still as a rock" (182). The effect, however, is to suggest the opposite of the deathlike insensitivity in which Anse lives. Jewel's rigidity masks the passionate love he feels for his mother and his outrage at the way everyone else is driving her toward her death, anticipating it, "sitting there, like buzzards. Waiting, fanning themselves" (14). The single monologue that reveals Jewel's feelings makes them very clear. He sees himself and Addie together fighting off the rest of the family: "It would just be me and her on a high hill and me rolling the rocks down the hill at their faces" (15). Much of our awareness of Jewel's presence is through others' perceptions of him. They see his rigidity, but only the mystical Darl recognizes the fury and despair that are beneath the surface. Other people's perceptions of Jewel are regularly mistaken. Cora Tull best exemplifies the limitations of the observers who base their judgments solely on appearances and never see what is real. Cora is quite certain about the accuracy of her understanding of Addie and her children's feelings about her, but although Cora's interpretations are coherent and logical, they are also uniformly incorrect.

Finally, in his characterization of the child Vardaman, Faulkner presents a basic confusion about life and death and about the animate and the inanimate, as if to show an exaggerated instance of what is a unifying theme for the novel. Vardaman's inability to accept the fact of his mother's metamorphosis from life to death is also a reflection of Faulkner's narrative problem, how to make such an event real, how to depict it convincingly. Addie's death becomes real for the reader cumulatively, as individual characters begin to act on the reality. In this way, by having a number of interior monologues that acknowledge her death in various ways, Faulkner obliquely achieves more verisimilitude than would be likely with a straightforward narrative account. Again, he has chosen an indirect strategy for depicting radical change.

Vardaman cannot begin to understand the loss. He knows only that his mother at one moment "is" and at another "is not." In the same way, the fish he has caught is no longer a fish either. It has been cleaned and cut up into "not-fish." Vardaman confuses the presences and absences of the fish, his mother, Doc Peabody, and Peabody's horses with cause and effect relationships. He actually blames the doctor for his mother's absence and comes to increasingly bizarre conclusions about identities: "My mother is a fish" (AILD 79). Even taking his age into consideration, Vardaman's behavior and perceptions seem insane and conceptually primitive. A world in which "is" and "is not" are the only two existential possibilities—a world in which "becoming" cannot be perceived or understood—is a grotesquely fragmented and incoherent place. Vardaman's acceptance of death involves an acknowledgment of the implications of change and of loss in his recognition of an absence strongly felt.

Vardaman's confusions are echoed in the perceptual idiosyncrasies of a number of characters in *As I Lay Dying*. Vernon Tull describes Vardaman as he holds his dead fish by anthropomorphizing it: "It slides out of his hands, smearing wet dirt onto him, and flops down, dirtying itself again, gapmouthed, goggle-eyed, hiding into the dust like it was ashamed of being dead, like it was in a hurry to get back hid again" (AILD 30). Anse does the same thing with the weather: "now I can see same as second sight the rain shutting down betwixt us, a-coming up that road like a durn man, like it want ere a other house to rain on in all the living land" (AILD 36). The obscuring of the boundary between animate and inanimate pervades this novel about death. Two distinctly human phenomena, sweating and bleeding, appear so often as attributes of inanimate objects that they begin to connote the creative force itself. Having just crossed a flood-swollen river, Tull envisions his home: "I could . . . see all the broad land and my house sweated outen it like it was the more the sweat, the broader the land; the more the sweat, the tighter the house because it would take a tight house for Cora, to hold Cora like a jar of milk in the spring . . ." (AILD 132). Again Faulkner is describing an object as being the result of the flowing of matter into new shapes. The creative flowing is the sweating, an appropriate figure of speech for a farmer to use; more importantly, it expresses in highly visual terms the effusiveness that characterizes flux in so many of Faulkner's descriptive passages. A large number of Faulkner's favorite words denote such flowing and elusiveness, that is, an indeterminacy of boundaries: "effluvium," "emanate," "redolent," "nimbus," "penumbra," "chiaroscuro," "twilight," "lambent," and so on. Surfaces in his fictive world continually flow beyond their boundaries, and what we are shown as readers often seems reminiscent of a more tangible and cohesive reality, felt somehow to have existed in the near past (or, rarely, about to exist in the future) and leaving its traces in the present moment. Thomas Sutpen's mansion is such a trace, *"the house which he had built, which some suppuration of himself had created about him as the sweat of his body might have produced some (even if invisible) cocoon-like and complementary shell"* (AA 138).

When objects do change in Faulkner's stories, he invariably chooses verbs of vision to describe the effect or the loss: "her peaceful, rigid face *fading* into the dusk as though darkness were a precursor of the ultimate earth, until at last the face seems to *float detached* upon it, lightly as the *reflection* of a dead leaf" (AILD 49, emphasis mine). Fading and dying are interchangeable processes in such passages. The failure of sight to control reality by reliably verifying the locations of boundaries and the failure of objects in reality to cohere and persist in time are inextricable. The perceptual problem reflects the ontological anxiety.

As I emphasized in chapter 1, important truths in Faulkner's stories are acquired through means other than sight—through intuition or hearing or smell, for example. The difference in effectiveness of sight as opposed to those modes of knowledge that are based on internal immediacy—with a notable blurring of subjective boundaries—reflects a world which both changes incessantly and yet, paradoxically, can in some sense be known. The sight of Addie's corpse and coffin does not convince the Bundrens of her death; instead, Vardaman drills holes in the coffin (one into her face) to allow her to "breathe." But the increasingly urgent presence of her decaying corpse, its irrefragable odor, causes the family members to realize that Addie and her corpse no longer have anything in common, that she is really gone and the corpse is a different thing entirely, to be disposed of as rapidly as possible.

The rhetoric of Quentin Compson's monologue in *The Sound and the Fury* is our final concern. It reveals the modes of perception of one explicitly preoccupied with the passage of time. Again, we have before us a slightly exaggerated instance of language reflecting a constant awareness of change and loss—by virtue of the obsessions that dominate everything Quentin does—but we see a perceptual style that, nevertheless, illuminates our understanding of more typical ways of looking at the world characteristic of even the omniscient narrators in Faulkner's stories. As Quentin experiences his world flowing out of control, his perceptions increasingly involve the spatializing of all of his sensations and thoughts in a manifest attempt to manage reality through the illusion of control that is innate to vision. Quentin, through Faulkner, virtually geometrizes the objects he encounters to control their relationships to one another and himself, and his story abounds with horizontal and vertical lines, oblique lines, bridges and lanes,[15] frames (mirrors, doorways, watch faces), enclosed spaces or spaces that feel like vacuums, and rhythmically regular segments of both time and space. The world itself undermines his efforts to keep things stable as it fragments, flows, and changes through time despite Quentin's vigilance. From the first words onward, Quentin's monologue expresses his struggle with time as he searches for timeless (that is, purely spatial, stable) modes of perception. Time is transformed into a place to be—"then I was in time again, hearing the watch" (TSAF 93)—but it is also his enemy because it is where change irrevocably occurs.

Quentin's radical spatializing is an attempt to reverse the effects of time,[16] specifically to undo the changes that have occurred in Caddy as her emerging sexuality has left him behind by totally changing their relationship. Quentin wants to recapture their reliance on one another and their intimacy by controlling and turning back time. As we shall see, he accomplishes this symbolically in his death.

Among the perceptions that dominate the monologue are those of Quentin's nihilistic father, Jason, which Quentin struggles unsuccessfully to deny. In Jason Compson's view, man is a pathetic combination of molecules and experiences doomed to fade quickly into anonymity and meaninglessness. Quentin tries to establish "importance" in his universe—a semblance of immortality, something that does not fade with time—but he is undermined by his father's vision of things: "Father was teaching us that all men are just accumulations dolls stuffed with sawdust swept up from the trash heaps where all previous dolls had been thrown away the sawdust flowing from what wound in what side that not for me died not" (TSAF 218); "Man the sum of his climatic [sic] experiences Father said. Man the sum of what have you. A problem in impure properties carried tediously to an unvarying nil: stalemate of dust and desire" (TSAF 153). Instead of flesh and blood, inanimate entities coalesce to form mankind.[17] There is no hope of achieving identity or importance in such a world, and we recognize in Quentin's efforts to reify such notions as honor, virginity, and his imagined incest with Caddy—all of which, because they are insubstantial, cannot fade—attempts to defy the dissolution that besets everything around him. Jason recognizes the illusoriness of such an imaginative control of one's perceptions: "you wanted to sublimate a piece of natural human folly into a horror and then exorcise it" (TSAF 220); "you are not thinking of finitude you are contemplating an apotheosis in which a temporary state of mind will become symmetrical above the flesh and aware both of itself and of the flesh it will not quite discard . . . you cannot bear to think that someday it will no longer hurt you like this" (TSAF 229).

The dissolution of Quentin's world is also suggested in the precariousness of his sense of self, especially evident in his relationship with his own shadow, that penumbral part of himself that he seems to regard as perversely having an existence of its own. A walk becomes an occasion to trick his shadow into merging with water or other shadows (TSAF 110, 114, 118, 166), to trample it into the pavement (118) and the dust (138), and to walk on its belly (119).[18] As a dimension of his own surface, Quentin's shadow is important because it shows us his preoccupation with control, literally with self-control. Perhaps his shadow, with its darkness and fluidity, represents the dark, soft, feminine aspect of Quentin and, as such, threatens him with a loss of his sense of himself; this meaning would certainly be consistent with our understanding of the similar dilemma in Joe Christmas. The shadow's easy merging with ground, water, trees, and other shadows through its softness and malleability suggests its affinities with the feminine. Quentin is only able to react to its flowing by asserting rigidity and control, by successfully "tricking" it. It is clear, though, that his shadow, as part of his surface, evades definition and management. It preserves its essential fluidity and, in doing so, serves as an appropriate focus for Quentin's absorption with the existence and potential annihilation of his own identity. His death plunges him into fusion with his shadow: "Niggers say a drowned man's shadow was watching for him in the water all the time" (TSAF 111).

Given Quentin's preoccupations in this monologue, it is not surprising that the descriptive passages here constantly play with boundaries and their various degrees of tangibility. Descriptions reminding us of figure-ground reversal are everywhere, as in the dozens of references to patches of sunlight and shadows. The two are, obviously, different aspects of the same phenomenon, an interaction of light and darkness. Faulkner even uses the image of a stencil to bring us both possibilities at once in an explicit figure-ground image: "The shadows on the road were as still as if they had been put there with a stencil, with slanting pencils of sunlight" (TSAF 149).

On other occasions Faulkner creates the effect of blurred experience by using synesthetic devices, either combining sound, smell, and sight or time and space or using one to describe the other. Thus, he speaks of *"the twilight-coloured smell of honeysuckle"* (TSAF 117) and of Gerald Bland, pulling his oars "in lonely state across the noon, rowing himself right out of noon, up the long bright air like an apotheosis, mounting into a drowsing infinity" (TSAF 149). He also describes the sound of a bell in terms of the space and silence that are its ambience: "When you opened the door a bell tinkled, but just once, high and clear and small in the neat obscurity above the door, as though it were gauged and tempered to make that single clear small sound so as not to wear the bell out nor to require the expenditure of too much silence in restoring it . . ." (TSAF 155). And again, "I ran down the hill in that vacuum of crickets . . . the air seemed to drizzle with honeysuckle and with the rasping of crickets a substance you could feel on the flesh" (TSAF 186). The effect he achieves by crossing these conceptual boundaries is the heightened intensity of the perception itself and a more convincing sense of experience, of reality. Each perception seems to be suspended among the possibilities implied by the multiple modes of perception that interact to reveal it, rather than being confined by a neat and finite correlation between the sense and the object perceived. In passages of this type we are encouraged as readers to accept the interchangeability of color, sound, smell, touch, and concept as evidence of the potency of experiences that are charged with meaning for his characters. This synesthetic description is consistent, too, with our earlier recognition that sound and smell are more potent indicators of reality for Faulkner's characters than sight. The interiority of sound and smell signifies subjectively that borders have been crossed (our own), just as synesthesia intensifies perceptions by providing that same illusion.

In the monologue preceding Quentin's, that of his retarded brother Benjy, a group of objects of various shapes, smells, and colors (especially red) comfort Benjy as substitutes for his sister Caddy,

whom Faulkner is careful to tell us Benjy "could not remember
. . . but only the loss of her" (TSAF 423). Benjy loves three things:
his sister, the pasture sold to pay for her wedding and send Quentin
to Harvard, and firelight. But the associations to these things are
virtually interchangeable. Firelight is "the same bright shape as
going to sleep" (TSAF 423), and Caddy smells "like when she says
we were asleep" (5). Her "hair was like fire, and little points of fire
were in her eyes . . . and Caddy held me" (88). Caddy often smells
"like trees" (8, 51, 58, 88), "like leaves" (5), and "like trees in the
rain" (22). Benjy's comforting bright shapes include the red cushion (like fire, warm, smells of Caddy), Caddy's slipper (warm,
smells of Caddy), and the pasture with its trees, leaves, and grass.
These are the reassuring smells, connected to his dim remem-
brance of the warmth she represented to him. Moreover, Benjy experiences all intense realities in terms of smell: death (Damuddy's),
sickness (Mother's), the cold, the perfume symbolizing Caddy's
unfamiliar sexuality, and the change as Caddy gets married. The
narrative associations reflect his intense, if primitive, perceptions
as he intuits the crucial truths about changes in his family.

Benjy is quite different from the cerebral, tormented Quentin,
yet his experiences prepare us for a corresponding group of associations that trigger Quentin's memories of his sister, associations as
complex with implications as Benjy's are straightforward. Quentin's thoughts about Caddy are fraught with many of the associations to the female that we encountered in *Light in August*. She and
women in general are linked with death ("the good Saint Francis
that said Little Sister Death, that never had a sister," TSAF 94),
with evil ("*they have an affinity for evil*," TSAF 119), with the potent smell of honeysuckle, which symbolizes sexuality as a pervasive and threatening presence, with the color red (blood, passion,
roses, "*Red print of my hand coming up through her face*," TSAF
166), and with the earth, the pasture, and water (Caddy up in a tree
with muddy drawers and lying in the river). The entire episode in
which Quentin walks near the river in Boston and tries to rid himself of the little Italian girl, whom he always addresses as "sister," is
interspersed with his memories of times when he and Caddy were
in or near the river near their home. These are sexually powerful
occasions when Quentin tries to make Caddy explain her relationships with men and her pregnancy and when they nearly complete
a mutual suicide (itself described in distinctly sexual terms).

The appeal of water, in fact, permeates Quentin's monologue. It is often in the background or in his thoughts. "I could smell the curves of the river beyond the dusk" (TSAF 211); "I can be dead in Harvard Caddy said in the caverns and the grottoes of the sea tumbling peacefully to the wavering tides" (TSAF 216–217). After his fight with Dalton Ames over Caddy, Quentin "couldnt hear anything but the water" (TSAF 201). There is reason to believe that the river and Caddy are closely associated in Quentin's mind, that indeed the river may stand for her in an important way. Earlier Faulkner stories reveal experiments with these psychic associations. In "The Kid Learns" Faulkner substituted for a death scene his young hoodlum protagonist's meeting of a girl with "eyes the color of sleep" who introduced herself as "Little sister Death."[19] In an allegory Faulkner wrote for his friend Helen Baird, a wounded knight frees himself from his companions Hunger and Pain by joining a maiden called "Little Sister Death" and then drowning himself in a river.[20] Other early stories reveal similar configurations: sisters and brothers, confusions of rivers with sleep or death,[21] and an innocent sleeping together of brothers and sisters that anticipates Faulkner's later, complex incestuous relationships in such works as *The Sound and the Fury* and *Absalom, Absalom!*[22]

William Niederland has written an essay entitled "The Symbolic River-Sister Equation in Poetry and Folklore," which suggests that this symbol derives from maternal images (water as the source of life) and birth fantasies. Both reflect the universal symbolism of water as "embracing life, birth, love, guilt, and death."[23] Niederland relates several mythical tales in which brothers and sisters, apparently as punishment for unconscious incestuous desires, are turned into rivers or into animals by drinking from rivers or (as in *The Mill on the Floss*) drown together or in which (as in Byron's *Childe Harold's Pilgrimage*) rivers carry a seductive appeal that only thinly disguises feelings for one's sister. He cites clinical material from several analysts affirming that such associations are common in the fantasies and dreams of patients.

Whether or not Faulkner has drawn from some mythic or psychic symbolic equation, he has in Quentin's case, as critic André Bleikasten has noted, made explicit connections between Caddy and rivers.[24] After he fights with Dalton Ames on a bridge over a river (over Caddy, as it were), Quentin is haunted by memories of the river at home, is fascinated with the river in Boston, and finally drowns himself there. It is both the end of his suffering and the culmination of his desire. His death acts out a fusion with Caddy: his desire for union with her and the annihilation of the personal distinctions that have made them separate people: "I will look down and see my murmuring bones and the deep water like wind, like a roof of wind, and after a long time they cannot distinguish even bones upon the lonely and inviolate sand" (TSAF 98). Psychologically, Quentin's suicide simultaneously fulfills his incestuous longing and allows him to punish himself for it. His love of death and his love for Caddy are nearly equated in this passage that emphasizes the tension he feels between maintaining a necessary distance (keeping the boundaries clear) and completely immersing himself into the other that he longs for: Quentin, "who loved death above all, who loved only death, loved and lived in a deliberate and almost perverted anticipation of death as a lover loves and deliberately refrains from the waiting willing friendly tender incredible body of his beloved, until he can no longer bear not the refraining but the restraint and so flings, hurls himself, relinquishing, drowning" (TSAF 411). Bleikasten shares my belief that "in Faulkner's fiction the perils of sex are often described in terms of engulfment, and drowning is a recurrent metaphor for the vertigo of lust."[25] Quentin's is an immersion into the Conradian "destructive element."

Quentin's death, moreover, and his trip through the secret waters to "the caverns and the grottoes of the sea" is reminiscent of another womb-like place that appeals to him: "When I was little there was a picture in one of our books, a dark place into which a single weak ray of light came slanting upon two faces lifted out of the shadow . . . It was torn out, jagged out. I was glad. I'd have to turn back to it until the dungeon was Mother herself she and Father upward into weak light holding hands and us lost somewhere below even them without even a ray of light. Then the honeysuckle got into it" (TSAF 215). Quentin sees himself and Caddy together in a dark place apart from their parents, not yet born, just as elsewhere he envisions himself and Caddy in Hell, encircled by flame but isolated and together. The honeysuckle (signaling the passage of time and the coming of sexuality) interrupts this fantasy, but Quentin's manner of dying has the effect of reversing time and sends him back to the state of uncreation represented when he and Caddy were in the dungeon of their mother. This remarkable visual image allows Quentin to be both undefined (= unborn = fused with Caddy = beyond the power of time to change them) and safely within a boundary (womb, dungeon, grotto, cavern, circle in Hell) that excludes the rest of the world. Then "it would be as though it had never been" (TSAF 220). "A quarter hour yet. And then I'll not be. The peacefullest words. Peacefullest words. *Non fui. Sum. Fui. Nom sum*" (TSAF 216).

In a passage near the end of Quentin's monologue, his multiple associations to Caddy appear, recur, and circle back on one another, creating an intensity that expresses Quentin's growing obsession with his sister and the centripetal movement toward fusion even of his perceptions as they foreshadow the manner of his death:

> I could see the twilight again, that quality of light as if time really had stopped for a while . . . and the road going on under the twilight, into twilight and the sense of water peaceful and swift beyond. . . . Honeysuckle was the saddest odour of all, I think. I remember lots of them. Wisteria was one. . . .
>
> . . . I could feel water beyond the twilight, smell. When it bloomed in the spring and it rained the smell was everywhere you didnt notice it so much at other times but when it rained the smell began to come into the house at twilight either it would rain more at twilight or there was something in the light itself but it always smelled strongest then until I would lie in bed thinking when will it stop when will it stop. The draft in the door smelled of water, a damp steady breath. Sometimes I could put myself to sleep saying that over and over until after the honeysuckle got all mixed up in it the whole thing came to symbolise night and unrest I seemed to be lying neither asleep nor awake looking down a long corridor of grey halflight where all stable things had become shadowy paradoxical all I had done shadows all I had felt suffered taking visible form antic and perverse mocking without relevance inherent themselves with the denial of the significance they should have affirmed . . .   (TSAF 209–211)

Twilight, which dominates this passage, is a recurring and important symbol in Faulkner's stories. Compressed into this one concept are many of the implications of his thoughts about transience and the nature of the lived moment. It suggests exactly the precarious coherence that characterizes the universe Quentin perceives, and *Twilight* was, in fact, the original title of Faulkner's *The Sound and the Fury*.[26]

Especially insofar as it presents a descriptive problem, twilight expresses the diffusion of qualities and imperfect clarity that are characteristic of the surfaces of objects in Faulkner's fictive world. The moment of twilight is at once intense and indeterminate. Visually, it is a fusion of light and dark, of white and black. Its essential feature *is* the flowing that carries it so quickly away, and the concept by which we think of the phenomenon "twilight" is one of those immobile entities that Bergson tells us typify the illusion that we are thinking of becoming itself. Twilight is quintessentially a blurring of sensations and boundaries, just as any subjectively experienced event is. Its fugacity also suggests the fundamental inexpressibility in words of events and personalities. A description of either an event or a person necessarily involves the illusions of unity and finitude that Bergson shows us are belied by experience. The flowing of temporal and spatial phenomena into one another is far closer to the experience of flux.

When we describe twilight, moreover, we can do it only by referring to what precedes and what follows it. In one case we have dusk; in the other, dawn. In this sense it is like any present moment in Faulkner's stories. Its intensity or essence is never described in isolation; Faulkner invariably provides a spatial and temporal ambience that confirms its meaning. In his prose, antecedents, subsequences, and environment become a major focus of narrative energy. Consequently, his descriptions are often more implied than actual as he exercises some of the possibilities of figure-ground techniques. Using synesthesia, oxymora, and neologisms, Faulkner is able to preserve the myriad possibilities inherent in the description of something as a direct description can scarcely do as well. The reader infers, connects hints, and fills in gaps to participate in creating the meanings Faulkner evokes. There are crucial absences everywhere in his stories, as we will explore more fully in the next chapter.

In a number of descriptive passages the moment of twilight and the experience of watching it are conjoined, quite appropriately, with an awareness of the sensations of sound and smell (as with Gail Hightower and Quentin Compson). The humming of insects, the murmuring of voices, the smell of honeysuckle (else-

where, verbena or wisteria), and a fading of the visual scene reinforce the sense of a relaxation of boundaries or distinctions, just as
they suggest a concomitant increase in subjective intensity. Vast
numbers of characters experience special insights, make decisions,
begin and finish journeys, go through crises, are born, and die at
twilight (both dawn and dusk) in Faulkner's world.[27] "It seemed
to him that he could see the yellow day opening peacefully on before him, like a corridor, an arras, into a still chiaroscuro without
urgency" (LA 104).

The titles of Faulkner's works are also revealing. In much of
his major fiction, his titles reflect an awareness of the evanescence
of moments and experiences: the hum of mosquitoes, the perva-
siveness of dust, haunting smells, the quality of a moment, the
quintessential and the intangible. The quality of light is an important focus: *Dark House* was the working title of both *Light in August*
and *Absalom, Absalom!*, evoking that dark, womblike place from
within which we have seen Hightower look out at twilight and
Quentin at weak maternal light. His titles often reflect times ("Dry
September," "Delta Autumn," "That Evening Sun," *Light in August*) because moments in time carry with them an elusiveness that
is central to his vision.

Twilight involves yet another meaning relevant to Faulkner's
perceptual style. It involves "a period of decline," the passing of
something into a lesser state, ultimately toward death or absence.[28]
In a larger sense, of course, Faulkner sees the Southern experience
itself as an attempt to cope with the degeneration of its culture following the Civil War, with the loss of what it was before 1861. But
throughout his fiction, as we have begun to see, it is the deteriora-
tion, fading away, death, and absence of important things that pre-
occupies Faulkner, his narrators, and his characters.

Significant Absences

was the saddest word of all there is nothing else in the world
its not despair until time its not even time until it was
The Sound and the Fury, p. 222

One of the prominent characteristics of Faulkner's prose is its thoroughgoing preoccupation with the past. Dominating his themes, it is reflected in his concern with the fate of the wilderness, the Old South, and the American Indian as aboriginal figure, as well as with the fates of individual characters, which so often hinge upon causes emerging from half real and half imagined pasts. His thematic preoccupation is reinforced by Faulkner's almost exclusive use of the past as his narrative tense, even in interior monologues disclosing the present thoughts of characters. Faulkner's depiction of the past is paradoxical, as our consideration thus far of his perceptual style would lead us to expect, but a consideration of the rhetorical devices through which he controls its narrative presentation will help us to understand the importance of both structural and thematic absences that pervade his works. And conversely, the significant absences in Faulkner's prose clarify the nature of his concern with time and transience and confirm that his well-critiqued passion for the past is made logically necessary by a very real preoccupation with loss.

As I suggested briefly in the previous chapter, there is an important difference between a world in which "is" exhausts the ontological possibilities and one in which experience is conceived both in terms of "is" and "was." As Henri Bergson suggests in *Creative Evolution*,[1] the use of the word "is" causes us to know that the existence of something is being asserted. This is a realm of simple predication, a present-tense world in which objects are known simply in relation to one another; objects that do not exist are irrelevant, neither present nor consciously conceived. It is a world without temporal referents. Faulkner approximates such a limited conceptual world fictively in his portrayal of Vardaman Bundren in *As I Lay Dying*. Apart from his youth and naiveté, Vardaman still

seems a nearly pathological figure so long as he is unable to reconcile the former existence of his (now dead) mother or the formerly
intact fish he has caught with the coffin and the cut-up fish pieces
now before him. "My mother is a fish," he concludes, for the mental juxtaposition of objects is his bizarre substitute for acknowledg-
ing temporal cause and effect. Things either are or they are not for
Vardaman, and his emotional task in the novel becomes the conceptual one of creating continuity by accepting the existence of the
past. Until he does, his perceptions are fragmented, and verbs of
simple predication dominate his speech.

With the addition of the dimension of time, the world is seen
more complexly, in terms of "is" and "was." To think "it was" is to
have memory. Inherently the verb "was" involves not-forgetting,
anticipation, and regret. As Bergson expresses it (writing on the
idea of "nothing"):

> The void of which I speak, therefore, is, at bottom, only the
> absence of some definite object, which was here at first, is
> now elsewhere and, in so far as it is no longer in its former
> place, leaves behind it, so to speak, the void of itself. A being
> unendowed with memory or prevision would not use the
> words "void" or "nought"; he would express only what is
> and what is perceived; now, what is, and what is perceived,
> is the *presence* of one thing or of another, never the *absence* of
> anything. *There is absence only for a being capable of remember-
> ing and expecting.* He remembered an object, and perhaps ex-
> pected to encounter it again; he finds another, and he expresses
> the disappointment of his expectation (an expectation sprung
> from recollection) by saying that he no longer finds anything,
> that he encounters "nothing." [2]

When such expectations are not realized, Bergson goes on, the recognition is one of "not so much thought as feeling, or, to speak
more exactly, it is the tinge that feeling gives to thought." [3]

A range of responses is possible to the absence thus acknowledged, from a disinterested recognition to deepest sorrow (or joy).
Faulkner's continual focus on the past and his use of the various
past tenses as he talks about people and things *present* in his fictional world suggest that the latter serve repeatedly as referents for
absent things. In a sense their importance resides in what they say
about what is missing: objects tend to be traces of absent objects,

and as readers we find our perceptions linked to those absent objects and their importance. Thus, in the ostensibly simple distinction between "is" and "was," we find much of the poignancy of Faulkner's thought. The word "was" becomes evidence that something no longer exists which once did exist. It reminds us of an absence *felt* as an absence, that is to say—in Faulkner's world—a loss. This affective quality is evident in Faulkner's description of Benjy Compson in the Appendix to *The Sound and the Fury*. Benjy is a timeless creature for whom present experiences are indistinguishable in vividness from his memories. He lives in a constant, subjective present tense, so his consciousness does not clarify for him that he misses Caddy: "Who lost none of them [the things he loved, reminders of Caddy] because he could not remember his sister but only the loss of her" (TSAF 423). Multiple traces of her—her slipper, the cushion, the smell of trees—torment him by somehow evoking that uncomprehended loss.

In its handling of time, Faulkner's rhetorical style again enacts a dialectic between flowing and control, between moments when semantic or structural boundaries are blurred and moments when, in contrast, they are vigorously asserted. He both depicts time as if it were all contained in any given present moment and treats moments of time as if they were discrete. The latter strategy is seen most clearly in the structures of his works. Faulkner emphasizes the pastness of the past by insisting upon boundaries that sever that past from present moments. Most conspicuously, he manipulates narrative sequences so that chronology is broken down and episodes are mixed up, deliberately confused with one another and juxtaposed in ways that obfuscate cause and effect. He fragments stories by experimenting with the number and type of narrators, interrupting one monologue with another, giving us information in little doses, overlapping two narrators' versions of the same event, and so on, to isolate events from one another by sheer discontinuity. As noted earlier, we cannot even determine the moment of Addie Bundren's death in *As I Lay Dying*, so continually is it anticipated, imagined, and remembered by others, a situation aggravated by the bewildering placement of her own monologue. Faulkner also leaves gaps so that many events are not described by anyone but instead are multiply implied by oblique references to them and by events that lead to or issue from them inexorably. Although all of Rosa Coldfield's narrative in *Absalom, Absalom!* is an anticipation of her revealing the nature of Sutpen's insult, she never describes it. Instead, Quentin Compson, who either imagines the event or was told about it quite apart from the recollections of this novel, projects his own account of the insult back into the gap left in Rosa's story. In *Light in August* Faulkner controls the evolution of Joe Christmas's story so that his birth comes last, next to the chapter in which Lena's baby is born, causing the two events to flow together imaginatively as the reader recognizes numerous elusive ways in which Joe's and Lena's fates seem intertwined. By manipulating episodes so that they are juxtaposed in ways that isolate them from their own consequences or that lead to unorthodox conclusions by virtue of associations set up in the reader's mind, Faulkner creates the illusion of discontinuity. His fragmentation of experience through such narrative strategies seems to insist on the boundedness of time and to control it by the very act of *being able to* isolate it into episodes and memories that are manipulable in a narrative sense.

But despite the obvious appeal for Faulkner of manipulating chronology in unorthodox ways, despite the consequent illusion of control, the flowing that is reality nevertheless pervades his writing. We perceive it—indeed, it is almost palpable—in various narrative devices that Faulkner has pushed close to their limits. Narrating an event, he regularly interrupts himself to recapitulate everything that led up to it, sometimes in great detail, sometimes by referring briefly to events elaborated elsewhere. The effect of his extensive embedding is one of such compression that as readers we are left a little breathless waiting for the new "fact" to be revealed. The clear implication emerges that all of the past is contained in every present moment, that everything is connected with everything else and boundaries have no meaning. In Bergsonian terms, there is only "becoming"—the plenitude of evolving experience. Faulkner reinforces this impression of the omnipresent past by repeating phrases, clauses, and words so that they accumulate nuances by virtue of their very redundancy. As a consequence, single words in Faulkner's prose take on unusually complex connotations.

The flowing together of experience is also intimated to the reader through Faulkner's dropping of capital letters and punctuation so that his thoughts are not separated in any visible way. Portions of *Absalom, Absalom!*, the fourth section of "The Bear," and the last part of Quentin's monologue in *The Sound and the Fury* of-ter good examples. The epigraph to this chapter is from the latter; punctuative ambiguities and Faulkner's refusal to clarify whether "was" is being used as a noun or a verb contribute to the passage's effectiveness by making each word seem to leap both forward and backward for meaning. In Faulkner's prose, when words have more than one possible referent, the ambiguity enhances the effect of fullness and evokes reverberations that perpetuate its rhythmic quality. His sentences are paradigms for giving a sense of every-thing—past, present, future—happening at once, and their flow-ing together or momentum seemingly threatens to take over in some of his unpunctuated, uncapitalized passages.

Faulkner also reflects the immanence of the past more tangibly when he describes a number of vividly recalled characters (remem-bered by present characters) as "ghosts," and in general because absent people, especially ancestors, exert inordinate influence on the lives of his characters. Such presences dominate a work like *Absalom, Absalom!*, which abounds with phantoms, ghosts, de-mons, "avatars," and other traces of people never even met by two of the narrators, Quentin and Shreve: " . . . the invoked ghost of the man whom she could neither forgive nor revenge herself upon began to assume a quality almost of solidity, permanence. Itself cir-cumambient and enclosed by its effluvium of hell, its aura of unre-generation, it mused . . ." (AA 13).[4]

Faulkner, then, maintains the dual nature of the past, seeing it simultaneously as fully contained and represented in the present moment and as separate, different, anachronistic, discontinuous, and importantly "other." His dual vision is an expression of an am-bivalence that allows him, even as he looks back over his shoulder to the purer past (Indians and their mythical closeness to nature, mules and blacks understanding one another in some prelapsarian manner), to insist with every story that the South's only hope is to abandon its unrealistic and archaic self-image.

To separate and connect moments of time in this way, to assert isolation and fusion, is to suspend our rational comprehension of the past between antitheses and to create what one critic has de-scribed as a "psychological oxymoron." Walter Slatoff sees all of Faulkner's stylistic traits as leading to such a suspension of our in-tellectual comprehension of what is happening.[5] One must agree. His conclusion is that the reader is thus led to understand intui-tively or emotionally the special kind of truth Faulkner describes.

As I shall show, however, the "suspension" is often vividly characterized as a space, a gap which the reader is meant to fill or complete in some actively creative way.

Many of Faulkner's sentences reflect an "either/or" pattern of
development consistent in its effects with those of oxymoronic
structures.[6] He is careful, however, to assure that as readers we can
supply the missing thought, as when he uses negation, saying, as
the Houyhnhyms in *Gulliver's Travels* phrased it, "the thing which
is not" to imply that which is. Consequently, his ideas are often expressed in terms of a "neither/nor" pattern in sentences that have
the effect of excluding the various possible definitions of what is
happening. There is a something unsaid that is meant—a crucial
absence. Variations of the pattern include Faulkner's description of
Judith Sutpen as "the daughter who was already the same as a
widow without ever having been a bride and was, three years later,
to be a widow sure enough without having been anything at all"
(AA 15), and such passages as these: "Beyond the unlamped wall I
can hear the rain shaping the wagon that is ours, the load that is no
longer theirs that felled and sawed it nor yet theirs that bought it
and which is not ours either, lie on our wagon though it does"
(AILD 76) and " . . . *about Jewel's ankles a runnel of yellow neither
water nor earth swirls, curving with the yellow road neither of earth nor
water, down the hill dissolving into a streaming mass of dark green neither of earth nor sky*" (AILD 48). Constructions of this type, by first
polarizing and then eliminating alternatives, reinforce the sense of
loss initially conveyed by the words themselves.[7]

Faulkner employs negation in many senses of the word, as
critics have long recognized.[8] He holds himself back, does not tell
his story, tells it slowly or obliquely, or stops entirely in order to
back up and start over again. His sentences are frequently tortu-
ous, and directly or through complicated qualifications they undo
things that have just been said. Both when Faulkner appends pre-
fixes and suffixes to words and when he nullifies whole clauses, he
negates what he has suggested ("*un*regret") or does so doubly ("*un*-
source*less*") or triply ("*nor un*insatiate"): "It was not that I could
think of myself as no longer unvirgin . . ." (AILD 165). His parallel constructions typically create tension among themselves by partially abrogating one another's meanings: " . . . the Grand Jury was
preparing behind locked doors to take the life of a man whom few
of them had ever seen to know, for having taken the life of a woman

whom even fewer of them had known to see" (LA 394). And his
very long sentences often have a rhythm created by a careful bal-
ancing of every element with its parallel, thus establishing relationships among multiple entities.

> . . . think of him, Bon, who had wanted to know, who had
> had the most reason to want to know, who as far as he knew
> had never had any father but had been *created somehow be-*
> *tween* that woman who wouldn't let him play with other chil-
> dren, and that lawyer who even told the woman whether or
> not each time she bought a piece of meat or a loaf of bread—
> two people neither of whom had taken pleasure or found pas-
> sion in getting him or suffered pain and travail in borning
> him—who perhaps if one of the two had only told him the
> truth, none of what happened would ever have come to pass;
> while there was Henry who had father and security and con-
> tentment and all, yet was told the truth by both of them
> while he (Bon) was told by neither.
>
> (AA 339–340, emphasis mine)

Even within constructions, Faulkner multiplies parallels and rhythmically balances nearly every phrase in the passage. Notice, as well,
the space "between" the woman and the lawyer, the undefined creative place.

As we read such a passage with its oscillating rhythms and referents, we enact the oxymoronic task of combining and comparing
things with one another. The doubling and multiplying implicit in
such parallel constructions remind us of the Medusa figure which,
in Freudian terms, denies the absence of something (there, the
phallus) by insisting that not only is there one of them, there are
several. Multiplying, in fantasy, has among other psychic functions
that of denying loss. In a world that feels painfully ephemeral, it
seems plausible that Faulkner achieves some illusion of permanence by saying things; as he writes them down, he can affirm their
existence before they go away: "nothing served but that I try by
main strength to recreate between the covers of a book the world as
I was already preparing to lose and regret . . . desiring, if not the
capture of that world and the feeling of it as you'd preserve a kernel
or a leaf to indicate the lost forest, at least to keep the evocative
skeleton of the dessicated [sic] leaf."[9] How much more convincing

this becomes when we recall the number of times he repeats wo
phrases, episodes, and entire stories, and how often he asserts t
two or more things happened or may have happened in his endless
parallel configurations. A number of passages in his prose and his
interviews affirm that for him the act of writing compensates for
a sense of loss. The following simile begins as an analogy and is
quickly elaborated into a fantasy of a kind of literary immortality:

> They were not looking at one another. It was like they were
> not even talking to one another but simply at the two empty
> reflections in the plate glass, like when you put *the written
> idea* into the anonymous and even interchangeable empty en-
> velope, or maybe into the sealed empty bottle to be cast into
> the sea, or maybe two written thoughts sealed forever at the
> same moment into two bottles and cast into the sea to float
> and drift with the tides and the currents on to the cooling
> world's end itself, *still immune, still intact and inviolate*, still
> ideas and still true and even still facts whether any eye ever
> saw them again or any other idea ever responded and sprang
> to them, to be elated or validated or grieved.
>
> (T 199, emphasis mine)

This fantasy suggests that for Faulkner writing involves filling an
empty space (envelope, bottle, page) with meaning and thereby denying the transience of things, especially of meaning itself. Importance seems to be the only possible immortality; it transcends even
existence. Thus, in Faulkner's stories we find concepts that by virtue of their importance alone have been reified: "What he was doing was simply defending forever with his blood the principle that
chastity and virtue in women shall be defended whether they exist
or not" (T 76). The ultimate irony of such sentences, of course, is
that the very words in which they are phrased so often, as here,
cancel out the possibilities that have just been suggested.

Other recurrent rhetorical devices of Faulkner's also reflect an
awareness of parallelism and multiplicity, of boundaries (affirming
or eradicating them), and of spaces. He uses synesthesia exten-
sively, just as he employs spatial and temporal terms to describe
one another, blurring the expected conceptual distinctions. Similarly, he creates new words by fusing existing words together—
"pinkwomansmelling," "Augusttremulous," "timespace," "not-

husband," "manhard." The elements of his neologisms stimulate one another and express a kind of intensity (subjectively, a tension) because boundaries have been so deliberately erased. I mean this in quite a literal sense, for Faulkner has abolished the space between words and left us to create or infer the meanings that such a move makes possible conceptually.

Faulkner often employs strict oxymora as well, whose elements contradict or modify one another to such degree that neither word reflects a clear meaning more closely than the other, so that determining the meaning requires an inference on the reader's part. Examples are "inflectionless finality," and "tranquil and astonished earth." He tends to use the expression "at once" before such phrases to deny us the simple solution of seeing one of the pair as semantically subordinate to the other.[10] Meaning is a function of both and yet neither of them. Faulkner also blurs the boundaries of clauses that parallel one another by using ellipsis so that, again, the flux of experience is conveyed and referents are not easily located: "Perhaps memory knowing, knowing beginning to remember; perhaps even desire, since five is still too young to have learned enough despair to hope" (LA 132). Only the rhythms and context of this sentence allow the reader to fill in the gaps and understand. Faulkner uses this strategy with whole sentences, as I have said, and with entire stories, as in *The Wild Palms*, where two separate plots serve as counterpoint to one another's meanings.

The techniques I have mentioned reflect the dialectic between flowing and control that comes from alternately focusing upon and eradicating boundaries between words and, by extension, the concepts they signify. As we turn to thematic issues, we recognize a number of concepts having to do with the boundaries or definitions that separate people and control their relationships to one another. An awareness of the vigorous boundedness of objects in Faulkner's world—for example, the perception of objects as shapes and containers—furthers our understanding of the sense of loss that boundaries can (and in Faulkner's stories do) defend against.

For the moment it will be helpful to remember a few of the instances in which Faulkner creates deliberate confusion about conceptual boundaries even while he maintains narrative control. Several of his characters have names that are both masculine and feminine (Bobbie in *Light in August*, Quentin in *The Sound and the*

Fury), and many share the same names with others to a degree that creates real bewilderment in sorting out events. These obfuscations suggest, on the one hand, androgynous thinking (as when characters are described as looking like the opposite sex)[11] and, on the other, temporal confusion or blurring. And yet misogyny simultaneously pervades Faulkner's work and reminds us of the psychoanalytic recognition that seeing or maintaining marked distinctions between the sexes may be a defense against the temptation to annihilate those distinctions entirely by identifying with women (a movement toward homosexuality). In Joe Christmas of *Light in August* there are hints of this ambivalence. In Faulkner I think it is accurate to suggest that the blurring of any boundary both produces anxiety and is, paradoxically, quite appealing. Consequently, a number of his stories are concerned in very particular ways with such themes as miscegenation, necrophilia, incest, androgyny, cannibalism, and homosexuality. Faulkner suggests an aberration—experienced both socially and emotionally as a crossing of forbidden lines—and then leaves us completely confused about whether or not it happened, as in "Dry September," which revolves entirely around an instance of apparently fantasized miscegenation. He qualifies, undoes, negates, or obfuscates to the point where it is equally plausible that an event did and did not occur.

Absalom, Absalom! provides the best examples. In it Faulkner suggests the violation of nearly every boundary that has been seen to sustain the individual's existence as a social being: life-death (murder, fratricide, cannibalism), male-female (seduction, incest, insult), male-male (homosexuality), and black-white (miscegenation). Then, as he distances events by giving numerous, incomplete, and contradictory narrative accounts, he manages to suggest that these events may not have happened at all. The "courtship" of Judith Sutpen and Charles Bon is only hypothetical, and the other events in the Sutpen history are all tenuous and unclear. Quentin and Shreve, thinking about them in retrospect, are described as "*creating between them*, out of the rag-tag and bob-ends of old tales and talking, people who perhaps had never existed at all anywhere" (AA 303, emphasis mine). Perhaps because so many boundaries are posited which cannot be allowed to relax, this is Faulkner's most amorphous, impalpable work. He manipulates the fantasy that they have been crossed at the same time that he denies it by obscuring and never verifying his material. The narrative, as words on paper, allows him to play with a dangerous "reality" while never letting it get out of control; it never becomes real enough to bring consequences.[12] Precisely these events are left undescribed and unverified, while their background or ambience provides support for nearly any inference we care to make.

The effect of these strategies on our reading of his stories is our sense at once of incompleteness and of myriad possibilities. There are gaps in our understanding which we fill imaginatively and which bring along with their bewildering aspects a sense of richness that is satisfying, perhaps because as readers we have helped to make them so.

Absences or gaps play numerous roles in Faulkner's fiction. Many of his stories, as I have mentioned, are characterized by absent central events (the murder in *Light in August*) and personalities (Caddy in *The Sound and the Fury*[13]). Notions of absence range from obvious spatial gaps that exist in objects to the absence of a particular experience in one's life; both have repercussions involving what is present and what is known in Faulkner's world. His sometimes odd definitions are one result. A gentleman, Jason Compson tells his son Quentin, is known by the books "*he has not returned*" (TSAF 99). In this obliquity, this being defined by something one has not done, we can discern a variation on the figure-ground reversal strategy I mentioned earlier.

Remarkably, Faulkner's notion of absence takes on both (1) a type of causality, being the occasion for other events, and (2) a tangibility that makes of absences places or things within which other things can exist. In *Absalom, Absalom!* a rapid series of absences or nonevents precipitates the turning point of the Sutpens' fate. Charles Bon repeatedly tries to interpret Thomas Sutpen's behavior in order to reach some conclusion about his father's thoughts about him:

> And the day came to depart and no sign yet; he [Bon] and
> Henry rode away and still no sign, no more sign at part-
> ing than when he had seen it first, in that face where he
> might (he would believe) have seen for himself the truth
> and so would have needed no sign . . . no sign in the eyes
> which could see his face . . . could have seen the truth
> if it were there: yet no flicker in them: and so he knew
> it was in his face because he knew that the other had seen

it there . . . by the fact that the father said nothing, did
nothing. (AA 320–321)

Seeing nothing becomes proof of what Bon had hoped to verify by
seeing: Thomas Sutpen's admission that he is Bon's father. Away at
college with Henry Sutpen, Bon writes to Judith:

> maybe he thought *If one of mine to her should come back to me
> unopened then. That would be a sign.* And that didn't happen:
> and then Henry began to talk about his stopping at Sutpen's
> Hundred for a day or so on his way home and he said all
> right to it, said *It will be Henry who will get the letter, the letter
> saying it is inconvenient for me to come at that time; so appar-
> ently he does not intend to acknowledge me as his son, but at least
> I shall have forced him to admit that I am.* And that one did
> not come either . . .   (AA 326–327)

Letters that are not returned and other letters that do not arrive
create for Charles Bon that absence of acknowledgment by his father which drives him to pursue an incestuous, miscegenetic marriage with Judith, an act which he must know presages his own
death. Characteristically, Faulkner undermines even this narrative
by having his narrator, Quentin, assert that "nobody ever did know
if Bon ever knew Sutpen was his father or not" (AA 269). Faulkner's use of absent things and events as causative agents means that
not happening, not knowing, and not seeing or hearing are important events in their own right.[14]

As we would expect in light of the material presented in chapter 1, Faulkner typically describes absences, whether places or nonevents, in spatial terms.[15] When Jack Houston is shot through the
stomach,

> he saw the blank gap, the chasm somewhere between vision
> and where his feet should have been, and he lay on his back
> watching the ravelled and shattered ends of sentience and
> will projecting into the gap, hair-light and worm-blind and
> groping to meet and fuse again, and he lay there trying to
> will the sentience to meet and fuse. Then he saw the pain
> blast like lightning across the gap. . . . Wait, wait, he said.
> Just go slow at first, and I can take it. . . . But it would not
> wait for him. It would not wait to hurl him into the void . . .
>   (H 217)

This is another example of figure-ground reversal as a descriptive technique, for Faulkner has given us a vivid, visual depiction of a critical space defined by what surrounds it. As the border between Houston's body and this inner space collapses, he dies and is hurled into another unbounded realm, the void beyond death (the final boundary). The spatial configurations in Faulkner's world seem to consist of objects carefully defined by boundaries that are in danger of collapsing or flowing away.[16] The movement of life is always toward flux and ultimate anonymity. Consequently, objects and spaces treated as objects are essentially perceived as shapes and often specifically as containers, holding (actually or potentially) other things. Outside the boundary of the known and the knowable is an inexpressible realm (e.g., the "void" beyond Houston's existence), but things also contain within them spaces to be filled or to be otherwise contended with.[17]

That absences are places or shapes waiting somehow to be filled is everywhere implicit in Faulkner's fiction. Objects that move continually leave behind them, as Bergson would say, the void of themselves: " . . . the men . . . hurled themselves onto the vacancy where a split second before he had been lying" (M 95); Addie's coffin "begins to rush away from me and slip down the air like a sled upon invisible snow, smoothly evacuating atmosphere in which the sense of it is still shaped" (AILD 92); and in a rather convoluted passage Faulkner tells us that if Eula Varner stops being a part of "Motion," she will "fill with her own absence from it [Motion] the aching void where once had glared that incandescent shape [herself]" (T 133). In other words, in motion, Eula leaves a void in space, and standing still, she leaves an absence in "Motion"; moreover, Faulkner defines her presence in one realm (space) in terms of her absence from another (motion), that is, as an absence that can "fill."

The tangibility of absences is also evident in Faulkner's use of accounts and ledgers as metaphors for getting and keeping things "even" in his world, that is to say, for defining and controlling things. When the Snopeses begin to proliferate in Jefferson, Gavin Stevens and V. K. Ratliff take upon themselves the task of saving the town by holding back their influx, and late in the Snopes trilogy, Faulkner tells us that "they—Jefferson—were holding their own. Because in that same summer, 1945, when Jefferson gained the new Snopes, Ratliff eliminated Clarence . . ." (M 295). Similarly, at the end of *Absalom, Absalom!* Shreve says: "So it took Charles Bon and his mother to get rid of old Tom, and Charles Bon and the octoroon to get rid of Judith, and Charles Bon and Clytie to get rid of Henry; and Charles Bon's mother and Charles Bon's grandmother got rid of Charles Bon. So it takes two niggers to get rid of one Sutpen, dont it? . . . Which is all right, it's fine; it clears the whole ledger . . ." (AA 377–378). And finally, Doc Peabody calculates absences to determine the moment when he can retire: "I'll be damned if I can see why I dont quit. . . . I reckon it's because I must reach the fifty thousand dollar mark of dead accounts on my books before I can quit" (AILD 42).

Getting things even again is a recurrent motive for Faulkner's characters; many of them seek a talion type of revenge for the wrongs they have endured or feel that such a revenge has been imposed on them: "I used to wonder what our father or his father could have done before he married our mother that Ellen and I would have to expiate and neither of us alone be sufficient" (AA 21). Still others pay for things with a particular type of suffering and feel that as a consequence they have earned an immunity from further pain. When Joe Christmas undertakes the ritual with the sheep's blood, he feels he has "bought immunity" (LA 176) from having to know about the fact of menstruation. And, tempted to become involved in Joe's struggle for survival, Gail Hightower thinks, "I wont! I wont! I have bought immunity. I have paid. I have paid" (LA 292), because of his own ordeal with the people of Jefferson. Again and again, paying for something is seen as the setting up of a boundary which ought to be secure.[18]

Some of Faulkner's characters actually exist in a state of immunity of one kind or another that provides them with a distinctly spatial insulation. We remember Wallstreet Snopes in the middle of the pony stampede; his immunity is a function of his age and lack of involvement in the world of women. Faulkner describes Judith Sutpen as existing in "that state where, though still visible, young girls appear as though seen through glass and where even the voice cannot reach them; where they exist . . . in a pearly lambence without shadows and themselves partaking of it; in nebulous suspension held, strange and unpredictable, even their very shapes fluid and delicate and without substance; not in themselves floating and seeking but merely waiting, parasitic and potent and serene . . ." (AA 67). Linda Snopes, after she becomes deaf, is described as "the bride of quietude and silence striding inviolate in the isolation of unhearing, immune" (M 230). Notice both the tangibility and the impermeability of the spaces in which these characters exist.

This type of insulation, however, is not only generated by silence or obliviousness. Whenever characters project a state of mind intensely, such spaces tend to be created, shields against experience. Narcissa Benbow "went on, surrounded by her grave tranquillity like a visible presence or an odor or a sound" (FD 110). Even noise, through its very din, produces the same effect: "perhaps the entire dilemma of man's condition is because of the ceaseless gabble with which he has surrounded himself, enclosed himself, insulated himself from the penalties of his own folly" (M 236). There is a sense in which Faulkner alternately uses the sounds of silence and of the continuous humming of insects and other such noises as environments into and out of which his characters move: "I could hear the sabbath afternoon quiet of that house louder than thunder" (AA 27).

But silence in Faulkner's world is not simply the absence of noise or even a quiet *place*. It has its own reality that can supersede other realities. For one thing, silence can absorb and hold on to noises or assert itself: "When you opened the door a bell tinkled, but just once, high and clear and small in the neat obscurity above the door, as though it were gauged and tempered to make that single clear small sound so as not to wear the bell out nor to require the expenditure of too much silence in restoring it . . ." (TSAF 155), and "The women sing again. In the thick air it's like their voices come out of the air, flowing together and on in the sad, comforting tunes. When they cease it's like they hadn't gone away. It's like they had just disappeared into the air and when we moved we would loose [sic] them again out of the air around us . . ." (AILD 86). Notice the "neat obscurity" in which the bell exists in the first passage, and the verbs "disappear" and "loose" in the second that emphasize the visual, spatial realm within which sound and silence coexist, the silence even for a time "absorbing" the sound.

Such passages suggest that silence and similar absences are not simply signifiers of nonexistence for Faulkner;[19] they are presences in their own right. As a consequence, they are manipulable and can even be negated or superseded by other, more negative things. Faulkner does not simply provide an antonym for the idea of remembering—forgetting. He gives forgetting its own kind of reality: "*He didn't even fail to remember me this time. He didn't even know me. He hasn't even bothered to forget me*" (ID 25–26). Just as there is something beyond forgetting, there is something beyond silence. "From the docks a ship's siren unsourced itself. For a moment it was sound, then it compassed silence, atmosphere, bringing upon the eardrums a vacuum in which nothing, not even silence, was. Then it ceased, ebbed; the silence breathed again . . ." (CS 896).

Faulkner gives a kind of reality to such concepts as silence because, it seems, those concepts thus become manipulable in the way any spatial, tangible object would be. To say that there is something more absent than the absence of noise is to make silence a relative thing, less purely a signifier of absence or loss. To treat silence like a container (capable of absorbing noise into itself, for example) is to make it finite, locatable, and to deny the very nothingness or absence of anything which would otherwise be its meaning. Faulkner postpones an acknowledgment of loss here, as always, by positing or emphasizing boundaries.

Absences in Faulkner's world are often perceived as shapes; this is as true of objects whose meaning to some degree involves their emptiness as it is of such notions as silence. People's houses, clothes, and bodies, in particular, are empty in ways that are expressions of the lives or personalities of their owners. Rosa Coldfield's self-alienation is reflected in her "small body . . . with its air of curious and paradoxical awkwardness like a costume borrowed at the last moment and of necessity for a masquerade which she did not want to attend" (AA 65). Faulkner uses images of clothes, shells, houses, and bodies interchangeably to suggest the quality of the emptiness or absence he wants to evoke. Ellen Coldfield Sutpen dies, "the butterfly of a forgotten summer two years defunctive now—the substanceless shell, the shade impervious to any alteration of dissolution because of its very weightlessness: no body to be buried: just the shape, the recollection, translated on some peaceful afternoon . . . into that cedar grove . . ." (AA 126). It is important to recognize that Ellen's body is depicted precisely as a trace, a "recollection" of what she was; it symbolizes both what she lost and the loss of her—the potential of a butterfly (a recurrent image for Ellen) and the actuality of an empty shape to be disposed of. Thomas Sutpen's house, reflecting his moral vacuity, is a "Spartan shell" (AA 39) with its own "incontrovertible affirmation for emptiness, desertion" (AA 85). And Quentin Compson, obsessed with figures from the past, sees his body as "an empty hall echoing with sonorous defeated names . . . He was a barracks filled with stubborn back-looking ghosts" (AA 12).

In one final example we can see the manner in which the perception of objects as containers has the effect of forestalling loss by insisting upon the substantiality and boundedness of something that threatens to go away. Vernon Tull, looking back toward his house at a time when he knows he is in danger of not returning there (because of a flooding river), sees his home and wife as receptacles:

> I could . . . see all the broad land and my house sweated
> outen it like it was the more the sweat, the broader the land;
> the more the sweat, the tighter the house because it would
> take a tight house for Cora, to hold Cora like a jar of milk
> in the spring: you've got to have a tight jar or you'll need a
> powerful spring, so if you have a big spring, why then you
> have the incentive to have tight, wellmade jars, because it is
> your milk, sour or not, because you would rather have milk
> that will sour than to have milk that wont, because you are
> a man.   (AILD 132)

This passage is typically Faulknerian in that, while ostensibly logical, it disintegrates from a rational point of view into nonsense.[20] Yet at the same time it clearly reflects the feeling of holding on that gives it its affective quality of longing and a fear of loss. The images move with a sense of urgency from the tenuousness and impalpability of sweat to the security of a "tight, wellmade jar."

Since Faulkner's visual imagination is impressionistic, he sometimes disregards the requisites of logic. At times a person's body is his "self" and what it contains feels alien: "In a strange room you must empty yourself for sleep. And before you are emptied for sleep, what are you. And when you are emptied for sleep, you are not. And when you are filled with sleep, you never were" (AILD 76). At other times the body is a shell or container for the person's essence, and the skin is seen as "the envelope in which [the sum of experience] resides" (AA 69). When this container is all there is—as with Ellen Sutpen, who moves through the stages of cocoon, butterfly, and finally empty shell—Faulkner is simply emphasizing all that was potential in Ellen that never happened. She

existed in only the most primitive sense of the word, with scarcely
an identity since she lived so purely in a world of illusion. In passages like the one above about Vernon Tull, a concentric image is
created in which the house contains Cora, who represents something sustaining like milk and who in turn contains the attributes
of that milk, "sour or not." Faulkner's descriptions of pregnant
women regularly suggest this idea of concentricity, of contained
spaces within containing spaces. Dewey Dell says of herself: "I feel
like a wet seed wild in the hot blind earth" (AILD 61). Pregnancy
is pure potential, the apotheosis of creative space.

In *As I Lay Dying* Addie Bundren's monologue is dominated
by perceptions of objects as shapes and by relationships conceived
in purely spatial terms: inside and outside, horizontal and vertical,
presences and absences. Addie's pregnancies, her terrible aloneness, and the violation of that aloneness are occasions for Faulkner
to employ his spatial imagination vigorously in creating a tension
between the flowing across boundaries that characterizes experience
(touching, intercourse, giving birth) and the boundaries themselves
that keep things in place and represent, paradoxically, both control
and death. Faulkner suggests the fragility of such boundaries in
this passage from *Absalom, Absalom!*: "*Because there is something in
the touch of flesh with flesh which abrogates, cuts sharp and straight
across the devious intricate channels of decorous ordering, which enemies
as well as lovers know because it makes them both—touch and touch of
that which is the citadel of the central I-Am's private own. . . . But let
flesh touch with flesh, and watch the fall of all the eggshell shibboleth of
caste and color too*" (AA 139).

Among the boundaries, the dead things, in Addie Bundren's
world, the most conspicuous are words. "Love, he called it. . . .
that word was like the others: just a shape to fill a lack . . . when
the right time came, you wouldn't need a word for that anymore
than for pride or fear" (AILD 164). Once again, we recognize the
paradox of a shape "filling" another shape, or the concentricity of
empty, bounded things. Words are "gaps in peoples' [sic] lacks"
(AILD 166); "sin and love and fear are just sounds that people who
never sinned nor loved nor feared have for what they never had and
cannot have until they forget the words" (AILD 165–166). To put
it differently, words do not simply fill lacks in people's lives; they
replace them. When you have words, you cannot have the absent
entities to which they refer, and when you have the experience it-

self, the word is extraneous.[21] The absences in people's lives are filled either by words or by doing, mutually exclusive possibilities. Moreover, for the most part, only the men in Faulkner's world need words (and concepts and rituals) to define the intensity of living. The young woman in "Delta Autumn" who has loved Roth Edmonds and had his child did not insist that he promise her marriage: "He didn't have to. I didn't ask him to. I knew what I was doing. I knew that to begin with, long before *honor I imagine he called it* told him the time had come to tell me in so many words what *his code I suppose he would call it* would forbid him forever to do" (GDM 358, emphasis mine).

The distinction between the male's need for boundaries (words, rituals, reified concepts) and the female's affinity with flowing, touching, doing, and being is a very real one for Faulkner's characters.[22] The very deadness of Addie's life with Anse Bundren is reflected in her perception of herself, him, his name, and their relationship as shapes: dead, bounded spaces. The boundedness that for males means security or autonomy (as with Vernon Tull and Roth Edmonds, above) is for women isolation and death—the absence of life, which they recognize intuitively as flux:

> I would think: Anse. Why Anse. Why are you Anse. I would think about his name until after a while I could see the word as a shape, a vessel, and I would watch him liquefy and flow into it like cold molasses flowing out of the darkness into the vessel, until the jar stood full and motionless: a significant shape profoundly without life like an empty door frame; and then I would find that I had forgotten the name of the jar. I would think: The shape of my body where I used to be a virgin is in the shape of a   and I couldn't think *Anse*, couldn't remember *Anse*. It was not that I could think of myself as no longer unvirgin, because I was three now. And when I would think *Cash* and *Darl* that way until their names would die and solidify into a shape and then fade away, I would say, All right. It doesn't matter. It doesn't matter what they call them.   (AILD 165)

Addie's sense of her aloneness is both vivid and paradoxical. Her isolation as a young woman causes her to beat her students in order to touch their lives with her own, and yet the pregnancies she later experiences are felt as violations, betrayals of her wholeness. The births restore her sense of herself as a space: "My aloneness had been violated and then made whole again by the violation: time, Anse, love, what you will, outside the circle" (AILD 164). In the long quotation above Addie perceives the spatial sense in which she used to be whole, a virgin, as reshaped by the presence of Anse into a new absence, the shape which Faulkner refers to by the space in his sentence and which Addie can only think of as the inverse of Anse's shape, that "shape profoundly without life."

But although her sense of wholeness and, paradoxically, of multiplicity ("I was three now") is established by the births, Addie has lost forever that shape or integrity or state of being which is virginity. Virginity is one of the most important abstractions in Faulkner's world, because it signifies a situation that is irretrievable once it has been lost. Indeed, the concept takes on importance, with few exceptions, only after it has been lost. Virginity is defined by the absence of a particular event; the presence of intercourse entails the absence of virginity. Thus, while aloneness and wholeness are recurrent states, virginity represents something so losable through the passage of time that it can symbolize the entire problem of transience: "[Henry Sutpen's] fierce provincial's pride in his sister's virginity was a false quantity which must incorporate in itself an inability to endure in order to be precious, to exist, and so must depend upon its loss, absence, to have existed at all" (AA 96). Elsewhere, Gavin Stevens explains more of the paradox:

That was it: the very words *reputation* and *good name*. Merely to say them, speak them aloud, give their existence vocal recognition, would irrevocably soil and besmirch them, would destroy the immunity of the very things they represented, leaving them not just vulnerable but already doomed; from the inviolable and proud integrity of principles they would become, reduce to, the ephemeral and already doomed and damned fragility of human conditions; innocence and virginity become symbol and postulant of loss and grief, evermore to be mourned, existing only in the past tense *was* and *now is not, no more no more*.   (T 202)

This passage reveals as well as any in Faulkner's stories the interrelationships of transience and immortality, of vulnerability and immunity, of mortality's essential fragility and the transcendent integrity of abstract "principles." Anything which is or becomes tangible in Faulkner's world (such as speaking the words aloud) becomes finite and thus part of the ongoing ephemerality of things, to be lost forever.[23] The only entities that successfully defy transience are intangible: "principles," which resemble Platonic forms in the sense that they transcend and survive any particular incarnation of what they stand for; and experiences or memories captured by a consciousness, remembered, and passed on (often symbolically) to other consciousnesses. In *Absalom, Absalom!* this preservative function is seen as Judith gives a letter from Charles Bon to Quentin's grandmother, who is nearly a stranger to her:

> And so maybe if you could go to someone, the stranger the better, and give them something—a scrap of paper—something, anything, it not to mean anything in itself and them not even to read it or keep it, not even bother to throw it away or destroy it, at least it would be something just because it would have happened, be remembered even if only from passing from one hand to another, one mind to another, and it would be at least a scratch, something, something that might make a mark on something that *was* once for the reason that it can die someday . . .   (AA 127)

Faulkner's favorite conception of the artist—what David Minter calls "a somewhat lush fin de siècle version of Romanticism's"—emphasizes this same desire: "The artist, he said, was a demon-driven creature, haunted by a foreknowledge of death and determined to leave a scratch on the wall of oblivion."[24]

An important consequence of the role of absences in Faulkner's prose is that objects that are present assume important referential functions. They serve as traces or reminders of absent things and embody the latter's meanings. A number of these artifacts are in the nature of containers that hold (literally or symbolically) formerly existing things. Letters and ledgers appear regularly as tenuous (because literally fading) traces of people and events:

> Beginning near the bottom of the final blank page, a column of names and dates rose in stark, fading simplicity, growing fainter and fainter where time had lain upon them. At the top they were still legible, as they were at the foot of the preceding page. But halfway up this page they ceased, and

from there on the sheet was blank save for the faint soft mot-
tlings of time and an occasional brownish penstroke significant but without meaning.

Bayard sat for a long time, regarding the stark dissolving
apotheosis of his name.   (FD 96)

Earlier I suggested that people's bodies, houses, and clothes
are interchangeable images when Faulkner describes them as lonely
or empty or haunted. Clearly, too, these various shapes—when
empty—are traces of the absent individual: the dead bodies of
Ellen Sutpen and of Addie Bundren, and Thomas Sutpen's empty
house must be contended with because of what they signify about
the missing person. Items of clothing are significant reminders of
the personality of their owner: " . . . there was something about a
man's destiny (or about the man) that caused the destiny to shape
itself to him like his clothes did, like the same coat that new might
have fitted a thousand men, yet after one man has worn it for a
while it fits no one else and you can tell it anywhere you see it even
if all you see is a sleeve or a lapel" (AA 245–246). Such items continue to exist in their own right apart from the presence of their
owners. Jody Varner wears his suits "every day and in all weathers"
and then sells them "to one of the family's Negro retainers, so that
on almost any Sunday night one whole one or some part of one of
his old suits could be met—and promptly recognized—walking the
summer roads" (H 7).

Traces, through their reference to absent things, often become
the focus of powerful feelings of longing. As an example, Gavin
Stevens, in his infatuation with Linda Snopes, sees himself as an
adolescent "at once drawn and terrified of what draws him . . . to
whom the glove or the handkerchief she didn't even know she had
lost, the flower she didn't even know she had crushed, the very
ninth- or tenth-grade arithmetic or grammar or geography bearing
her name in her own magical hand on the flyleaf, are more terrible
and moving than ever will be afterward the gleam of the actual
naked shoulder or spread of unbound hair on the pillow's other
twin" (T 208–209). In this particular quotation, we see that an
ironic reversal has taken place in which the trace has become more
precious than the absent beloved. This is because of Gavin's deep
ambivalence toward Linda ("at once drawn and terrified of what
draws him"), a masculine response to woman's sexuality that is

typical among Faulknerian males. As we will see near the end of chapter 4, it is possible that the trace is valued *because* it signifies an impossible longing, that attainment of the desire would plunge the character too terrifyingly back into the world of change and loss.

Favorites among such objects as those mentioned above—a trace that is distinctly also a container—are the empty shoes of absent people.[25] Benjy Compson clings to the slipper that Caddy has left behind, and Linda Snopes Kohl's thoughts are similarly focused as she mourns for her husband: "It's the rest of it, the little things: it's this pillow still holding the shape of the head, this necktie still holding the shape of the throat that took it off last night even just hanging empty on a bedpost, even the empty shoes on the floor still sit with the right one turned out a little like his feet were still in them and even still walking the way he walked, stepping a little higher with one foot than the other like the old-time Negroes say a proud man walks—" (M 251).

Everywhere in Faulkner's stories we encounter objects that tell stories, confirm our hypotheses, or entail messages about people who are absent. Charles Bon's photograph of his mistress and child is a message to Judith not to mourn him (AA 359). The sprig of verbena in "An Odor of Verbena" and the strand of hair in "A Rose for Emily" are remnants of passions that no longer exist. The recurrent smell of honeysuckle or wisteria,[26] the vast number of footprints or other traces of fugitives—these types of artifacts appear repeatedly. There is scarcely a Faulkner novel that does not contain a hunting story; always there are runaway horses, slaves, architects, criminals, or cows, or wild animals being hunted, and dogs or blacks following tracks and scents. The object as trace is a powerful aspect of Faulkner's imagination.[27] After Flem Snopes leaves his job as superintendent of the power plant, he is seen sitting and looking at its shape "standing against the sky above the Jefferson roof-line—looking at his own monument, some might have thought. Except that it was not a monument: it was a footprint. A monument only says *At least I got this far* while a footprint says *This is where I was when I moved again*" (T 29).

Even people occasionally serve as traces—when they symbolize something to someone else rather than being accepted fully as human beings. Rosa Coldfield speculates about what Thomas Sutpen could have wanted from her and knows that it was only her ability to help him restore Sutpen's Hundred after the Civil War and to give him a male child: "*my presence was to him only the ab-sence of black morass and snarled vine and creeper to that man who had struggled through a swamp with nothing to guide or drive him—no hope, no light: only some incorrigibility of undefeat—and blundered at last and without warning onto dry solid ground and sun and air . . . I was that sun, or thought I was . . .*" (AA 166–167).

Presences that signify absences—traces—pervade Faulkner's writing and prevent the reader's (or character's) consciousness from ever being able to extricate itself from an awareness of loss, since what each object signifies is so much more important than what it simply is. Not only does Faulkner perceive absences every-where around him; he concentrates the fact of loss by reifying it: "*he realized that there was more in his problem than just lack of time, that the problem contained some super-distillation of this lack*" (AA 279). Thus, a major role of boundaries in Faulkner's fictive world is that of dealing with impending loss, of containing things.

Words, which Addie Bundren describes as boundaries and shapes and finite entities, are the vehicle that Faulkner relies upon —by the act of writing his novels—to bring the world of flux under some semblance of control. The problem with objects themselves is that they fade and die; they are hopelessly mutable. But words are potent symbols and as such can simultaneously stand for and sur-vive the objects they refer to. Faulkner often refers to the role his writing plays in symbolically capturing the essence of an experience by creating a trace of it. Words are traces, ways of saying "No to death":

> So he who, from the isolation of cold impersonal print, can
> engender this excitement, himself partakes of the immortality
> which he has engendered. Some day he will be no more,
> which will not matter then, because isolated itself invulner-
> able in the cold print remains that which is capable of en-
> gendering still the old deathless excitement in hearts and
> glands whose owners and custodians are generations from
> even the air he breathed and anguished in; if it was capable
> once, he knows that it will be capable and potent still long
> after there remains of him only a dead and fading name.[28]

Like all symbolization, writing fills a space both physically (the pages of a book, the space occupied by a sculpture) and psychically (the need or absence that prompted the creativity in the first place). Its presence thus both substitutes something for the loss, undoing it or compensating for it *as* a loss, and serves as a trace (reminder, symbol) of the lost entity. It is both comforting and a reminder of the need for comfort. Like the writing of most authors, Faulkner's serves this function: it is a trace of something absent which it signifies.[29] What makes Faulkner's perceptual and narrative styles distinctive are the particular structures and themes that define the quality of the sense of precariousness of his universe: the rhythms of boundedness and containment vis-à-vis flowing and empty spaces. Spaces that in other writers—equally conscious of containment, let us say—might be the physical counterparts of promises, representing infinite possibilities, are for Faulkner ways of holding on to things; they deny and prevent loss.

Faulkner's elaborate narrative structuring offers him what reality never allows: control of the presences, the absences, and the symbols that unite them.[30] His concern with spaces is reflected as Faulkner defines and then fills in the space of his universe, Yoknapatawpha County, peopling the county with successive generations or with invasions of Snopeses; as he stylistically fills in gaps by selectively releasing new information to his readers; and as he creates ultimately spatial concepts, objects, and patterns[31] which he fills or defines, but rarely completely, so that there is still a sense of space which the reader helps imaginatively to complete. His delineation of spaces and assertions of boundedness provide him with the imaginative security, as it were, both to tolerate and give expression to the appealing flux of experience, which in life carries with it significant amounts of anxiety because it so essentially involves loss. Yet the structuring, the themes, and the words themselves are evidence of the concern about transience and loss that they have been created to control. They at once gratify, reflect, and perpetuate a need.

Chapter Four
"The Terror of History": Faulkner's Solution

If you could just be translated every so often, given a blank,
fresh start, with nothing to remember. Dipped in Lethe every
decade or so . . .   *Flags in the Dust*, pp. 339–340

Locked as he is into a conception of time that is linear, sequential,
and historical, modern man has not often been able to escape the
fear that human suffering is arbitrary. In his prose Faulkner continually expresses the futility and poignancy of human attempts to
overcome the inexorable passage of time, which changes things
even as they come to have meaning and, thus, constantly renews
humankind's experience of aloneness and loss. Faulkner's imagination of this experience, too, is a spatially conceived one: "Being
dragged by time out of a certain day like a kitten from a tow sack,
being thrust into another sack with shreds of the first one sticking
to your claws" (FD 339). The struggle both to depict the quality of
life being lived through time and to deny or undo through fictional
devices and the fact of his writing the loss implicit in time's passage
leads to much of the paradoxical quality of Faulkner's writing. It
especially accounts for many of the tensions and dialectical rhythms
we experience at different levels of discourse: fictive events that
seem determined or compelled juxtaposed to those of mythic transcendence; fluctuations between moments when visual boundaries
are emphasized (control, containment) and others when they dissolve; and dualistic and figure-ground imagery that polarizes concepts so that we understand them in terms of their opposites. Perceiving time itself as a spatial phenomenon, a "corridor" or "road"
beyond which there is nothing, Faulkner writes in ways that enable
him imaginatively to deal with the threat of meaninglessness. Mircea
Eliade terms this unalterability of time "the terror of history," and
our concern in this chapter is to look at another of the techniques
through which Faulkner fictionally expresses and copes with this
ontological and psychological anxiety.

   We have seen that the strong spatiality of Faulkner's vision has
as one of its effects an illusion of control of the objects in his fictive

world. His focus on the edges, surfaces, and boundaries of things (including concepts) seems intended to give them a tangibility that denies their evanescence. We have also seen that on highly structured occasions, Faulkner may obscure boundaries to suggest fusion and flowing. A variation of this same rhythm between flowing and control is evident in Faulkner's use of ritual and myth in his stories. I use the words "ritual" and "myth" in a general sense: ritual as an acting out of meaning which is myth; myth as the source and justification of ritual. Each is capable, paradoxically, of existing independent of the other.

Both Faulkner as writer and his narrators and characters enact (verbally or physically) the structured and repetitive behavior of rituals that sometimes lead beyond themselves to a form of unstructured experience and sometimes, instead, end as a mindless repetition of acts that no longer have meaning. It is the structure and control of ritual that occasionally make possible a moment of transcendence because an individual will come to feel control and trust vis-à-vis environments that lend themselves to such encounters. Mircea Eliade has elaborated this dimension of ritual at length,[1] especially as it functions in initiatory rites such as those we find in Faulkner's hunting stories. In *Go Down, Moses* especially, we find all of the elements of initiatory rituals that Eliade and others have documented. Such rites have the effect of offering new beginnings to the participants, new identities and relationships with the wilderness and the men who are their peers.

In terms of Faulkner's own imagination, it is helpful to recall that rituals often specifically act out a crossing of boundaries. They mediate the tensions involved in encountering anxiety-producing things at close range, and they legitimize the merging of normally separate things. As David Minter emphasizes in his biography, Faulkner controlled his personal life through a continual oscillation between involvement and detachment, and ritual became part of his strategy for "controlling and delimiting his interaction with his world."[2] Faulkner developed "highly stylized relationships with acquaintances, friends, and relatives alike—a habit that lasted a lifetime."[3] As we shall see when looking at his texts, whether temporal or spatial movement is involved, Faulkner uses ritual to guide the crossing of established boundaries and movement among definitions that otherwise segment the various aspects of our lives. Initiations into manhood and funerals would be examples of changing definitions through time (childhood/adulthood, life/death) and marriages and football games of changing spatial relationships. Dilemmas and tensions among human beings are frequently avoided or eased through ritual, and in its absence chaos may result, as, for example, in a lynching that precedes—and thus prevents—a trial.

As Eliade has explained, in the mythic imagination (whether in primitive groups of people or in the vision of the mythic artist) ritual behavior has as one of its functions a recreation of the moment of creation itself. By acting out the behavior of early gods or mythic heroes, people can recreate sacred time as well as sacred space—a time and space removed from mundane existence and transcending it by literally creating new beginnings. For primitives, behavior is meaningful and real *only* when it reenacts such sacred events, only when it is behavior that is interpretable in terms of the meaning of myth.[4] A ritual reestablishes the original experience and its meaning, bringing order out of chaos and, in doing so, giving the participant a genuinely new beginning. This renewal obliterates merely temporal events because the god or hero is present once again and begins "history" anew. The belief in a new beginning is appealing because it has the effect of denying history; human difficulties can be seen as part of a larger plan or as having been erased by the new creation. The belief explains the sense of rebirth or, at the least, of release or refreshment that accompanies successful enactments of ritual. In Faulkner's stories, the mythic experience of rebirth or release is sometimes healthy and at other times perverse (Joe Christmas's release into death, Quentin Compson's suicide).

Faulkner's characters are often locked into time and tortured by that fact. Incapable of focusing on either a present or a future that could eradicate the past, deny its omnipresence and its implications, Faulkner can suggest the possibility of escape only by positing timeless, transcendent events. Intuitively he turns to myth, an immortal and boundless realm, to undo the effects of his otherwise time-entrapped perceptions of reality. He evokes the mythic through two devices: (1) by suggesting in both the form and content of his fiction that ritual behavior can lead to a state in which boundedness does not obtain and (2) by creating characters who embody a mythic defiance or transcendence of boundaries. The rhythm of flowing and control emerges here as a rhythm between ritualized repetitions (actions, narratives, syntax) and release into unstructured experience. We have already noted one example of this in chapter 1, where Faulkner's recitation of "The Phoenix and the Turtle" was seen as signalling the start of a bout of heavy drinking. In Faulkner's stories, the relaxation of boundaries is nearly always an event preceded by a structured preparation, a ritual, whether his own in a linguistic structure or a character's in repeated behaviors or thoughts.

It is noteworthy that Faulkner has chosen the wilderness as the location for his most striking presentations of ritualistic behavior because of the multiple meanings he assigns to the wilderness as a symbol. It represents for him a massive unknown entity, awesome in its darkness, impenetrability, and serenity. The wilderness, as earth and as Other, is feminine.[5] And because it is, it evokes the same anxieties that women often do:

> He was quite comfortable. But mainly he was off the ground. That was the danger, what a man had to watch against: once you laid flat on the ground, right away the earth started in to draw you back down into it. The very moment you were born out of your mother's body, the power and drag of the earth was already at work on you; if there had not been other womenfolks in the family or neighbors or even a hired one to support you, hold you up, keep the earth from touching you, you would not live an hour. And you knew it too. As soon as you could move you would raise your head even though that was all, trying to break that pull, trying to pull erect on chairs and things even when you still couldn't stand, to get away from the earth, save yourself. . . . Then you are a man grown, strong, at your peak; now and then you can deliberately risk laying down on it in the woods hunting at night; you are too far from home to get back so you can even risk sleeping the rest of the night on it. Of course you will try to find something, anything—a plank, boards, a log, even brush tops—something, anything to intervene between your unconsciousness, helplessness, and the old patient ground that can afford to wait because it's going to get you someday . . .
>
> (M 402)

Since men are powerless against the threat of earth and women, it is not surprising that they should perform rituals in attempting to deal with them. Rituals do not work with women, however,[6] and

genuine communication between men and women is rare in Faulkner's stories. Because they refuse to cooperate in rituals or to play
"by the rules," women are unpredictable, so they seem insidious
and threatening. Rituals are more likely to be effective, though, in
the wilderness. Each winter, then—when the woods are dormant
rather than fertile—men leave women and civilization behind and
go into the woods together. There they live out the rituals that help
them to feel reaffirmed as men and as hunters. They hunt, drink,
and share experiences around a campfire, and then return home to
their responsibilities, renewed.[7]

In this world of masculine companionship women represent
all of the things that oppress men and keep them bound—commit-
ment, anxiety, unpredictability. Consequently, when a woman enters a hunting camp, the value of the ritual is annulled; something
like chaos results. In "Delta Autumn" the woman who has had
Roth Edmonds's child follows him to the hunting site. Although
she has not come to make any demands, her presence completely
disrupts the camp and its occupants. Even Isaac McCaslin finds it
difficult to be sympathetic to her, so thoroughly does she represent
the exigencies of time to him—racial guilt, sexual exploitation, and
his family's culpability through the years. She brings profane time
with her, reminders of past behavior and present responsibility,
and the trip is rendered a failure. As if to symbolize the breakdown
in the structured rapport between man and the wilderness, Roth
kills a doe. He violates the code requiring men to provide for future
game; he dishonors himself as a hunter and thwarts the possibility
of finding transcendence in a successful enactment of ritual.

The measure of the men's acceptance of the meaning of their
rituals is reflected in the degrees of their competence as hunters and
woodsmen. Ultimately, the best of them go beyond the rituals to
mystical encounters with the wilderness. Their mastery of the rituals seems to equip them to face and withstand the enormity of the
unknown, and the rites maintain their relationship with that unknown, one of trust, acceptance, and mutual integrity.[8]

The most fully drawn successful relationship with the wilderness is that of Isaac McCaslin. Between his childhood and his old
age (the two alone are periods in a man's life of relative freedom
from destructive entanglements with women), he finds annual renewal in his pilgrimages to the woods. Ike remains childless and has
only the briefest of sexual relationships with women (GDM 311–

315), and one senses that his distance from women as well as his refusal to assume possession of inherited land give him a special integrity that sets him apart from his peers: "he would marry someday . . . but still the woods would be his mistress and his wife" (GDM 326). Ike's encounters with the woods begin with hunting near Jefferson with Sam Fathers as a boy; he learns to handle a gun and stalk small game and then moves through successive stages of competence in his mastery of hunting. His progress is measured in terms of his increasing ability to be self-sufficient, to find his way back from ever-deeper parts of the wilderness, and to encounter the woods and its larger game unscathed. In "The Old People" Ike kills his first buck and later sees a huge, mythical buck that represents the pride and magnificence of the wilderness itself. Only a few characters are allowed this particular vision, which is described as a mystical feeling of unity and a reciprocal acknowledgment of worth. There are Ike and Sam Fathers and, years earlier, McCaslin Edmonds, who have achieved a special understanding of the deep woods and are able to recognize the deer's meaning, and childlike Boon Hogganbeck, part Indian (thus, closer to nature than white men, in Faulkner's view), who never killed anything except a sitting squirrel and who does not understand what he has seen. Both of the events of this day reflect moments when the ritual of waiting on one's stand for game to appear brings about a mystical encounter; the bucks are like apparitions, and time is suspended: "the wilderness watched them pass, less than inimical now and never to be inimical again since the buck still and forever leaped . . . still out of his instant of immortality the buck sprang, forever immortal . . . Sam had marked [Ike] forever one with the wilderness which had accepted him" (GDM 178). The sense of a new beginning for Ike is very strong both here and in "The Bear," in which Ike's relationship with the woods reaches maturity.

As Ike learns more about the woods in which the bear, Old Ben, lives, he surpasses any need for Sam's guidance and faces the lessons of the woods alone. Once, searching for Old Ben, he realizes that his gun and, later, his compass and watch are barriers keeping them apart. They represent intrusion, aggression, and a need for control implied in the measurement of time and space, so he leaves them behind. Losing track of the boundaries that measurement defines, Ike quickly becomes lost; then he and the bear see each other across a glade resembling one of Eliade's sacred

spaces: "[The bear] did not emerge, appear: it was just there, immobile . . . dimensionless . . . It didn't walk into the woods. It
faded, sank back into the wilderness without motion" (GDM 209).
The language in passages like this and the previous one suggests
that the emphasis on boundaries that usually characterizes Faulkner's descriptions has been displaced by an imagery of fusion in
which the buck, the bear, the wilderness, and even Ike are identified with one another, seen as a single entity, if only for that mythic
moment. This annihilation of distinctions is attained through ritualized encounters with the awesome Other.

After Sam and Old Ben have died, Ike visits the woods to see
their graves and encounters a six-foot snake. He remains unharmed,
however, even though the snake represents all of sin (therefore,
womanhood)[9] and danger, the essential threat of the unknown:
"the old one, the ancient and accursed about the earth, fatal and
solitary and he could smell it now; the thin sick smell of rotting
cucumbers and something else which had no name, evocative of all
knowledge and an old weariness and of pariah-hood and of death"
(GDM 329). The snake simply moves away, not seeing Ike as an
enemy. Ike's relationship with the wilderness gives him something
that Gail Hightower, Joe Christmas, and other Faulknerian males
long for—an immunity from harm by the Other, whatever its
form. His annual trip to the woods imbues Ike with the will and
strength to withstand his wife's and society's insistence that he accept the land he has been bequeathed. The notion of possessing
land has become senseless to him for it violates the integrity that
ought to exist between man and the earth.

The purity of Ike's rapport with the wilderness is unusual.[10]
More often, we find men using the annual trips into the woods to
refresh themselves and to share a masculine camaraderie that offers
them some degree of spiritual strength. Faulkner experienced this
special feeling about his own hunting trips. The language he uses to
describe these occasions is often densely poetic. He enjoys evoking
the primordial relationship of man and nature before civilization
imposed its limitations on our lives. Thus, characters who encounter
nature with dignity and competence win all of Faulkner's respect.

The cyclical nature of annual trips into the woods and the renewal they bring are paralleled elsewhere in Faulkner's stories by
cyclical movements that lead, sometimes compulsively, to other

kinds of escape or transcendence. A return to the same place may, paradoxically, offer freedom, however bizarre its form. Compulsion may end in a form of release. The characters who perform these repetitive behaviors are Faulkner's male protagonists, who are often introspective and who tend to suffer from tortured perceptions. Among them, we find Joe Christmas's circular journey especially vivid: "he is entering it again, the street which ran for thirty years. . . . It had made a circle and he is still inside of it. . . . 'But I have never got outside that circle. I have never broken out of the ring of what I have already done and cannot ever undo'" (LA 321). Joe's travels, given a deterministic tone through the circular imagery, bring him at the end of his life to his grandparents' hometown, and his suffering is finally ended in a death described explicitly as a release from boundedness (LA 440). His compulsive search for a sense of identity that fits what he feels about himself is consistently described in terms of circularity and entrapment. In Joe's behavior (see chapter 1) we recognize the essentially ritualistic nature of compulsive behavior, the repetition again and again of acts which try to undo or deny our anxieties and yet which, failing, reestablish them.

In *Light in August* Faulkner splits his central figure—the scapegoat—into two characters, one who acts (Joe) and one who ponders the implications of his suffering (Gail Hightower). As scapegoats, these two share the same experiences as victims of the town's refusal to accept them as they see themselves; instead, the townspeople have judged and persecuted them according to narrow, stereotyped expectations. Both Joe and Gail act out rituals in an attempt to buy themselves "immunity" from further intrusions into their lives (LA 176, 292). I have already mentioned Joe's killing of the sheep and sinking his hands into its blood in order to "undo" the knowledge of menstruation; later he is shaken at the discovery that, despite his ritual, menstruation exists as a reality that will affect his life. The failure of the ritual leads, almost predictably, to boundary chaos as Joe, once again, vomits at an encounter with female sexuality. Joe kills Joanna Burden precisely when their ritualized encounters cease and she becomes unpredictable, terrifying him with her insistence that he pray with her. After his wife's death, Hightower tries to continue to define himself as the town's minister by returning every week to his empty church, until the town locks its doors to him. Then his repeated twilight visions offer him a new identification as he equates the meaning of his life with the moment of his grandfather's heroic death in a cavalry charge (LA 465). Joe's behavior brings on his lynching, which releases him from the "cage" of his flesh (LA 151), while in Gail's final vision, the "wheel" of his thinking is seen as rushing out of him, spinning out (circularity again) to fuse with his mystical reliving of the "dying thunder of hooves" (LA 467). In death and in hallucination, respectively, these characters find respite from body- and time-bound perceptions that have made their existences a series of repeated, compulsive acts.

Just as Faulkner split Joe Christmas and Gail Hightower into active and cerebral aspects of a personality made the scapegoat to a community's failure of sympathy, he also split apart Bayard Sartoris and Horace Benbow, two young men who return from World War I in *Flags in the Dust*.[11] Tormented by memories of his brother, who died in that war, Bayard is nevertheless essentially an active figure, always physically moving in self-destructive, compulsive ways. Horace is less active and more poetic; he muses over the meaning of the war he and Bayard have just left behind. Horace sees in his sister Narcissa a serenity that seems to him the antithesis of the horrors of war. He relates to her and to the peacefulness that he imagines as radiating like a space around her as to a safe place, a haven. Reminiscent of the images discussed in the last chapter, Narcissa represents containment, holding, and safety: "his sister beyond the lamp from him filled the room with that constant untroubling serenity of hers in which his spirit drowsed like a swimmer on a tideless summer sea" (FD 189). The images in Horace's thoughts about Narcissa recur, with minor alterations, as their relationship continues. Returning to the thought of her is itself a peace-restoring act for Horace. As he gradually begins to live his life apart from her, Horace blows a number of glass vases (remember their role as containers and traces) to hold on symbolically to the comfort she represents. Faulkner also has Horace allude frequently to Keats's "Ode on a Grecian Urn," in which a painted urn is doubly a container (both inside and on its surface) of evoked, missing things.[12] Horace describes the beauty of both the vases and his sister in identical language, names one of the vases "Narcissa," and keeps it on his nightstand, acts confirming their identity in his imagination.

Horace's ruminations about his sister and the war express themselves in repeated thoughts and images and in the relatively innocuous pastime of blowing vases, all of which allow him to turn away from the war to "the meaning of peace" (FD 177). Bayard, in turn, acts out his obsession with war and death in overtly physical ways; he races feverishly around the countryside in anything that might kill him in his attempt to get his mind off of the loss of his brother John. Aunt Jenny recognizes that, in a manner characteristic of Sartorises, Bayard is enacting a death wish: "Did you ever hear of a Sartoris dying from a natural cause, like anybody else?" (FD 108). Horses, cars, and planes, as we have seen, are ubiquitous in Faulkner's stories as means to a type of freedom and exhilaration and as vehicles of escape from women. First on a horse, then in a car, and finally in a plane Bayard acts out self-destructive behavior that eventually reaches its goal. He is knocked unconscious after a desperate ride on a stallion (FD 141) and later goes off a bridge while racing in his car (FD 231). On both occasions Narcissa sees him when he is hurt and recognizes the deathlike peacefulness he has achieved: "the pallid, suddenly dreaming calm of his bloody face from which violence had been temporarily wiped as with a damp cloth" (FD 159); "On the pillow Bayard's head lay as she had remembered it on that former day—pallid and calm, like a chiselled mask brushed lightly over with the shadow of his spent violence" (FD 243). For Bayard, furious speed—ritualistically pursued—temporarily obliterates his obsession with the terrors of his own history.

When his grandfather dies of a heart attack during one of Bayard's frenzied drives, Bayard tries to escape the enormity of his guilt by going out into the country to stay with the MacCallum family for a while. In sharing hunting and friendship with this group of strong and competent men, he finds a brief reprieve from the consequences of his behavior. As a hunting trip, however, this one is a distinct failure, for Bayard is preoccupied with his guilt and the unalterability of his grandfather's death. They fail to find the fox they have been hunting, for Bayard has tainted the ritual. When he realizes that the MacCallums will soon know about what has happened, he leaves Jefferson behind. In Chicago he deliberately and drunkenly accepts the challenge to fly a completely untested airplane, and in it he dies, completing the cycles he has acted out for months.

The compulsion in Bayard that leads to these aggressive acts is based in his inability to stop imaginatively reenacting the moment of John's death. Ever since John crashed in his airplane, Bayard's failure to save him as he fell through the sky has haunted him. He relives the event repeatedly until finally his imagination supplies that variation that alone would have satisfied him. In other words, he ritualistically repeats the act until he gets it right, adding the detail which would have made the event bearable: "he recalled that morning, relived it again with strained and intense attention from the time he had seen the first tracer smoke, until from his steep side-slip he watched the flame burst like the gay flapping of an orange pennon from John's Camel and saw his brother's familiar gesture and the sudden awkward sprawl of his plunging body as it lost equilibrium in midair; relived it again as you might run over a printed tale, trying to remember, feel, a bullet going into his body or head that might have slain him at the same instant" (FD 368–369). If Bayard had died at the same moment as his brother, he would not have had to remember it and to suffer the loss. Bayard takes advantage of the first situation that allows him to live the solution discovered in his imaginative reenactments of John's death. He kills himself by flying a plane no one should have flown, reminding us that he had tried to keep John himself from flying the Camel, "that goddam little popgun" (FD 44).

Although Bayard's behavior vividly reflects his pursuit of death, Faulkner makes it clear through Aunt Jenny's reflections that his compulsive recklessness is a trait carried in male Sartorises' genes. Faulkner seems to need to account for the disappearance of a family—much like his own—which represents in his fiction a good deal of what it meant historically to be a Southern aristocrat: nobility, a sense of honor, courage. Yet the wry sarcasm and sorrow with which Aunt Jenny muses on their history reveals the anachronistic quality of their search for a "Sartoris heaven in which they could spend eternity dying deaths of needless and magnificent violence while spectators doomed to immortality looked eternally on" (FD 94). That this search for a transcendent experience was sometimes successful is seen in Faulkner's description of young John and Bayard's repeated pranks. After he has parachute-jumped from a balloon and landed in a brier thicket, young John has "on his scratched face that look of one who has gained for an instant a desire so fine that its escape was a purifaction, not a loss" (FD 74).

The words "not a loss" affirm the appeal of a mythic moment "so fine" that the finitude of life—the very context within which loss exists—can be momentarily surpassed.

Childish pranks have always had an element of defiance in them. They deny the expectations and responsibilities implicit in family life, specifically through the women who historically have always told little boys what to wear and how to behave. These acts are rituals of defiance and freedom just as going into the woods to hunt ultimately is. As the last quotation confirms, such behavior sometimes indeed leads to a new beginning in Eliade's sense. But Bayard's death, too, must finally be seen as a comparable, if perverse, release from time-bound existence.

Another of Faulkner's tormented protagonists is the schoolteacher Labove in *The Hamlet*, who is obsessed by his desire for eleven-year-old Eula Varner. Labove teaches school to earn the money to attend the university at Oxford, and during the four years leading to his degree, he gradually realizes that Eula has become an obsession: "for the first time he said the words, I will not go back. It had not been necessary to say them before because until now he had believed he was going on" (H 117). Even when he is finally admitted to the Bar and able to begin his law career, he cannot free himself of her. "And he could not do it. Even with that already forty miles of start toward freedom and (he knew it, said it) dignity and self-respect, he could not do it. He must return, drawn back into the radius and impact of an eleven-year-old girl . . ." (H 113).[13]

Eula's sexuality is so tangible a quality that Labove recognizes that it will conquer him. The narrator expresses Labove's fascination and terror in classic castration imagery: "And he did not want her as a wife, he just wanted her one time as a man with a gangrened hand or foot thirsts after the axe-stroke which will leave him comparatively whole again" (H 118). Eula is both a paragon and parody of the feminine. Labove's helplessness in dealing with her is typical of masculine attempts to cope with the enveloping softness and fluidity that are perceived as being so threatening in women. In Labove we see obsessive thoughts and rituals that never work; instead, he is trapped by his inability to do anything but repeat them.

In showing us the vicissitudes of Labove's obsession Faulkner uses language suggesting a basic difference between the cyclical *rhythms* that characterize the experience of women and the circular/cyclical *patterns* acted out by men.[14] We find him describing the

same activity (here, eating), on the one hand, as an example of serenity: "He could see her, even smell her, sitting there on the
school steps, eating the potato, tranquil and chewing . . ." (H 116);
on the other hand, it can reveal compulsion: "Then day would
come and he could rise and dress and eat the food which he would
not even taste. He had never paid much attention to what he ate
anyway, but now he would not always know that he had eaten it.
Then he would go and unlock the school and sit behind his desk
and wait for her to walk down the aisle" (H 118). Eula's behavior is
expressed through participles, verbs expressing *being* and implying
(if obliquely) her contentment with the present moment.[15] Labove's behavior, in contrast, is seen as compulsive, cumulative, and
focused on a single event in the future or the past: her presence.
The repeated use of the word "and" heightens the ritualistic tone of
his actions: "Yet still he stayed on. He stayed for the privilege of
waiting until the final class was dismissed and the room was empty
so that he could rise and walk with his calm damned face to the
bench and lay his hand on the wooden plank still warm from the
impact of her sitting or even kneel and lay his face to the plank,
wallowing his face against it, embracing the hard unsentient wood,
until the heat was gone. He was mad. He knew it" (H 119).

When she surprises him at her bench, he goes after her, and
they wrestle. Labove's language evinces a particularly destructive
vision of the underlying nature of the male-female encounter:
"That's what it is: a man and a woman fighting each other. The hat-
ing. To kill, only to do it in such a way that the other will have to
know forever afterward he or she is dead" (H 121). Instead of love
(the dissolution of subjective boundaries), there is hatred focusing
on the need to fight and leave an impact on the other in an aggressive touching that will confirm her otherness, her separateness,
once and for all. Sex and death are equated as a radical fusion or
blurring of boundaries; after them, as we saw in Joe Christmas
when he paid off the prostitutes, separateness must again be established so that the other remains distinct from the self and, moreover, so that the other "know[s] forever afterward" that she is so.

When Eula leaves, Labove goes to his desk, sits, stares at his
clock, and meticulously measures the time and distance necessary
for Eula's brother, Jody, to get to the schoolhouse and avenge her
insult. He minutely imagines Jody's arrival, his coming in "at once,
vindicated at last after five years of violent and unsupported convic-

tion. That would be something, anyway. It would not be penetration, true enough, but it would be the same flesh, the same warm living flesh in which the same blood ran, under impact at least—a paroxysm, an orgasm of sorts, a katharsis, anyway—something" (H 122). This fantasy recurs in Faulkner's stories as brothers and "lovers" of women encounter one another in battle replete with sexual overtones, as if the woman herself is so threatening as to be paralyzing, whereas her brother/suitor represents a desirable male surrogate. This imaginative escape into homosexual fantasy is essentially an escape from overwhelming anxiety about the female.

The final "death" that Eula inflicts on Labove is that she doesn't even mention the incident to her brother: "She never told him at all. She didn't even forget to. She doesn't even know anything happened that was worth mentioning" (H 126). Completely defeated by being unable to touch her life, Labove leaves town.

Although few other women in Faulkner's prose approach Eula's intensity as a representation of the female, they all share to differing degrees the mystery, the unapproachable feminine knowledge,[16] the unpredictability, and the threat of the unknown that cause men to feel helpless and anxious and to attempt to use rules, rituals, and words to deal with them. When Labove tries to think of the man who could be Eula's husband, he thinks of him as a "crippled Vulcan to that Venus, who would not possess her but merely own her by the single strength which power gave . . . as he might own . . . a field, say. He saw it: the fine land rich and fecund and foul and eternal and impervious to him who claimed title to it, oblivious, drawing to itself tenfold the quantity of living seed its owner's whole life could have secreted and compounded, producing a thousandfold the harvest he could ever hope to gather and save" (H 118–119). The sexual encounter of the farmer and his field is analogous to that between male and female. Man is helpless in the face of the eternal, fecund, impervious Other, whether field or wilderness or woman.

So much of the behavior of men in Faulkner's fictive world seems ritualistic that it is tempting to attribute the word "ritual" to all of their repeated behaviors. There is, however, a special tone of drivenness and a need for control that characterize the motivations implicit in many of their activities and create that compulsive orientation toward the other that we call ritual. Even the comical account of Uncle Buck and Uncle Buddy McCaslin's relationship with their Negroes involves such an acting out of ritual as a way of maintaining a needed illusion of control. Buck and Buddy live in a log house on their plantation and have housed their Negroes in its large, unfinished manor house:

> It didn't have any windows now and a child with a hairpin could unlock any lock in it, but every night when the niggers came up from the fields Uncle Buck or Uncle Buddy would drive them into the house and lock the door with a key almost as big as a horse pistol; probably they would still be locking the front door long after the last nigger had escaped out the back. And folks said the Uncle Buck and Uncle Buddy knew this and that the niggers knew they knew it, only it was like a game with rules—neither one of Uncle Buck or Uncle Buddy to peep around the corner of the house while the other was locking the door, none of the niggers to escape in such a way as to be seen even by unavoidable accident, nor to escape at any other time; they even said that the ones who couldn't get out while the door was being locked voluntarily considered themselves interdict until the next evening. Then they would hang the key on a nail beside the door and go back to their own little house . . .   (UNV 53)

This bit of country humor appealed to Faulkner, for he repeated the same anecdote on several occasions. It is a fantasy of successful containment and control. The fact that everyone seems aware of the farcical nature of the control doesn't alter the fact that *as a game with rules*, it works. Neither group violates the trust and predictability established by the ritual. This is a type of cooperation that is, of course, impossible to exact from a woman, whose sexuality makes her the inscrutable apotheosis of Other.

The feeling evoked by the compulsive behavior of Faulkner's characters is one we are all familiar with. A number of them spend inordinate amounts of time thinking obsessively about lost objects (as Quentin's thoughts about Caddy) or about threatening ones (Gavin Stevens's thoughts about the Snopeses) and acting in ways that ritualize their encounters with others, thereby reinforcing boundaries and asserting control. Perhaps the most thoroughly compulsive interaction with reality is seen in Quentin Compson, whose thoughts and actions lead inexorably to the fusion of perceptions that precedes his death (see chapter 2). As an adult, Quentin repeatedly counts and measures things, recreating the futility of his attempts in grade school to count the seconds until the bell rang; he was never able to come out even with the bell (TSAF 109). He re-imagines every event that tortures him about his past with Caddy, even including a fantasy in which he is present to prevent Dalton Ames, Caddy's lover, from being conceived: "If I could have been his mother lying with open body lifted laughing, holding his father with my hand refraining, seeing, watching him die before he lived" (TSAF 98). On the day he dies, Quentin meticulously avoids know-ing the exact time through an elaborate process of not looking at watches and clocks. Sometimes he imagines himself or his father as God (TSAF 152), who by saying that something is so or is not so can make it be true: "if i could tell you we did it would have been so and then the others wouldnt be so and then the world would roar away" (TSAF 220). Quentin's obsession with time is persistent; his thoughts repeatedly return to the same place—his awareness of his own loss and his attempts to undo that loss.

In an excellent study of the mutual influences between Quen-tin's dual roles as narrator and character, John Irwin has discussed the relationship between repetition and the motive of revenge. He shows us that these notions are analogous in the work of Nietzsche and Freud as well as Faulkner. Irwin asks, "Why does the attempt to repeat the past and correct it turn into the revenge against time?" [17] Then he has Nietzsche respond in a quotation from *Thus Spoke Zarathustra*:

> To redeem those who lived in the past and to recreate all "it was" into a "thus I willed it"—that alone should I call redemption. . . . Willing liberates; but what is it that puts even the liberator himself in fetters? "It was"—that is the name of the will's gnashing of teeth and most secret melan-choly. Powerless against what has been done, he is an angry spectator of all that is past. . . .
> . . . This, indeed this alone, is what *revenge* is: the will's ill will against time and its "it was." [18]

Repeated thoughts and actions that attempt to redo or undo events from the past are the ones we recognize as compulsive or ritualistic; their objective is control. In the focus upon "it was," we see that

Nietzsche and Faulkner share a conception of human tragedy in which "man in time can never get even, indeed . . . that the whole process of getting even is incompatible with time." [19]

The motive of getting even that characterizes compulsive behavior is revealed on numerous occasions other than the overt, circular, compelled activities of protagonists who are explicitly preoccupied with their own suffering. As elements of plot itself, the following types of events are common in Faulkner's stories: characters who see themselves as expiating others' sins, that is, paying for or undoing them; characters who try to buy "immunity" by acting in accordance with others' expectations; characters who try to trick one another to get even for the fact that they have themselves been tricked in poker games, horse trades, with seeded money, and so on; characters who track one another down in order to get even for real or imagined insults (like Mink Snopes); characters who brood over ledgers and over measuring and counting things (Harry Wilbourne); and characters who incessantly sue one another. It is the motive of somehow getting even with others or with the past or with life itself that sets these behaviors apart as compulsive ones. Moreover, it is nearly always men in Faulkner's stories who behave this way. As opposed to their own modes of interaction and perception, men assume that women, blacks, the earth (wilderness, field), and their counterparts exist beyond such concerns.

We have seen, then, that on particular occasions Faulkner's males perform ritualized repetitions that sometimes briefly free them into a timeless, boundless state of mind and at other times fail and end simply as repeated, ineffectual behavior. [20] The second major way in which Faulkner evokes the possibility of transcending time-entrapped existence is his implication that certain characters simply embody an insouciance toward such concerns. Basically, these characters are those felt to be most distinctly Other by the Southern white male consciousness that constitutes the narrative voice in Faulkner's novels. The most obvious, dominant example, of course, is women, and more precisely, women whose felt sexuality plagues the men fascinated by it. Because of the basic way in which perceptions of and assumptions about women permeate the perceptual patterns I have been describing, I will turn to the other figures first and return finally to draw some conclusions about

Faulkner's depiction of women and about how these figures are all related.

In an earlier chapter I mentioned that the very young seem to live in a safe space, for they are not yet sexual beings. Like them, the very old are far less tormented than Faulkner's typical protagonist. The reason that young boys and old men share in this degree of serenity, this untroubled state of mind, is their distance from sexual entanglements, whose tensions and anxieties—based in a pronounced consciousness of vulnerability to the other—are never far from Faulkner's imagination. Perhaps for this reason, the relationships between young siblings or friends, between the very old, and between the young and old are among the most relaxed and sympathetically drawn in Faulkner's prose. In these characterizations alone, we find poignancy, warmth, innocence, and loyalty, whereas between men of sexual age, rivalries over women, money, or land are far more characteristic. The elderly, while obviously not immune from physical harm, as little boys often are in the stories, reveal humor and an acceptance of things that make them more endearing and realistic than some of Faulkner's tortured protagonists. Theirs is not a transcendence of time as much as it is a peacefulness born out of their no longer needing to be aware of it; as old man Falls expresses it, "I aint got so much time I kin hurry it" (FD 245). It is because these figures are asexual and thus not obsessed with boundedness, differences, and control that affection between them is possible. Their indifference to boundaries (time, measurement, and so on) is reflected in their living very comfortably alongside the ghosts from their own pasts. "As usual old man Falls had brought [the long dead] John Sartoris into the room with him. Freed as he [John Sartoris] was of time, he was a far more definite presence in the room than the two of them [Falls and his friend, Old Bayard Sartoris] cemented by deafness to a dead time and drawn thin by the slow attenuation of days" (FD 5). The old often live imaginatively in the past and confuse present events with past ones; they eradicate the boundaries of history by living it constantly. Miss Jenny called Narcissa's infant son "Johnny" and recalled "anecdotes of that other John's childhood, until at last Narcissa realized that Miss Jenny was getting the two confused" (FD 409).[21]

Two of Faulkner's elderly characters are given special narrative attention as figures of strength and integrity. Sam Fathers and

Lucas Beauchamp are represented as having overcome to various degrees the fact of their mixed blood and the social barriers that this fact entailed in the turn-of-the-century South. Both figures take on mythic qualities by virtue of a pride that enables them to overcome racial expectations and implicitly demand and receive respect from their white peers.

Sam Fathers receives much of his stature as a character through his special rapport with the wilderness and his transmission of his knowledge and capacity for empathy to others, notably Isaac Mc-Caslin. Sam is the son of a Chickasaw chief and a quadroon slave, and Faulkner makes much of the tension caused by his three racial legacies. As we by now expect of him, Faulkner conceives this conflict in visual terms, as if Sam's racial components remain distinct as three types of blood in his veins: " . . . one day he found out that he had been betrayed, the blood of the warriors and chiefs had been betrayed . . . through the black blood which his mother gave him. Not betrayed by the black blood and not wilfully betrayed by his mother, but betrayed by her all the same, who had bequeathed him not only the blood of slaves but even a little of the very blood which had enslaved it; himself his own battleground, the scene of his own vanquishment and the mausoleum of his defeat" (GDM 168). Faulkner depicts Sam's Indian blood as purely a source of pride, and he implies that both the Indian and black blood carry some primitive or intuitive form of knowledge that was "tamed out of [white] blood so long ago that we [white people] have not only forgotten [it], we have to live together in herds to protect ourselves from our own sources" (GDM 167). But despite the dignity implicit in his heritage as the descendant of an Indian chief and despite his own integrity and mystical understanding of the wilderness, there is something which limits Sam's life, even if it manifests itself only as an ongoing awareness of something in his racial past. It is noteworthy that this single limitation is described in such decidedly visual terms. Sam becomes a "battleground," a defined but somewhat open space, which evolves into a "mausoleum," a constricted space that, moreover, signifies death. The ambiguity of containment is suggested here; that which can mean security and control becomes, for a strong, nearly autonomous character, staticity and death.

Despite his serenity and strength, then, Sam is kept from being a truly transcendent figure by the fact in his history that keeps him locked into time. In Sam's eyes is the knowledge of bondage, "that for a while that part of his blood had been the blood of slaves" (GDM 167). For Faulkner it is a cage that he did not know he was in until he recognized its antithesis—freedom. Then, like a caged animal (see the epigraph to chapter 1), he smelled the cage he had always lived in.

The characterization of Lucas Beauchamp is worth comparing with that of Sam Fathers, for in it Faulkner attempts to give the same situation—miscegenation—a more positive resolution. In Lucas we find a more vigorous assertion of identity than we did in Sam Fathers. Lucas views himself less as a Negro than as the oldest McCaslin descendant living on the McCaslin plantation. His portion of white blood brings him not the knowledge of the sin of slavery, but pride based in his romanticized vision of the greatness of old Carothers McCaslin, his white grandfather. His dignity is partly a function, too, of the integrity of his relationship to land, reflected in his attitude toward farming: "he approved of his fields and liked to work them, taking a solid pride in having good tools to use and using them well, scorning both inferior equipment and shoddy work . . ." (GDM 42). This detail and Lucas's refusal to submit to white people's expectations about him contribute to making him a figure of dignity and integrity.

Lucas's sense of his own value allows him to act like any other man. He is "the Negro who said 'ma'am' to women just as any white man did and who said 'sir' and 'mister' to you if you were white but who you knew was thinking neither and he knew you knew it but who was not even waiting, daring you to make the next move, because he didn't even care" (ID 18). Consequently, the motives of white people become focused, especially in *Intruder in the Dust*, on one thing: "*We got to make him be a nigger first. He's got to admit he's a nigger. Then maybe we will accept him as he seems to intend to be accepted*" (ID 18). This is reminiscent of Mottstown's relationship with Joe Christmas (LA 331), but Lucas's sense of himself is quite different from Joe's.

Lucas treats Zack Edmonds, another (white) grandchild of Carothers McCaslin, as his peer "to the extent of intending to kill him" (GDM 44) in their confrontation over Lucas's wife, Molly. Lucas later sees himself as fully equal, if not superior, to Zack's son Roth Edmonds, because "there was that quarter strain not only of white blood and not even Edmonds blood, but of old Carothers McCaslin himself, from whom Lucas was descended not only by a male line but in only two generations, while Edmonds was descended by a female line and five generations back" (GDM 104). Genealogical closeness to the source and descent through the male line signify, for Lucas, the greater status.

When Faulkner discusses Lucas's mixed blood, he retains the terminology we found in descriptions of Sam Fathers, but he abandons the antagonistic metaphor:

> Yet it was not that Lucas made capital of his white or even his McCaslin blood, but the contrary. It was as if he were not only impervious to that blood, he was indifferent to it. He didn't even need to strive with it. He didn't even have to bother to defy it. He resisted it simply by being the composite of the two races which made him, simply by possessing it. Instead of being at once the battleground and victim of the two strains, he was a vessel, durable, ancestryless, nonconductive, in which the toxin and its anti stalemated one another, seetheless, unrumored in the outside air.
>
> (GDM 104)

Faulkner has chosen to make Lucas a genuinely transcendent figure who, unlike the other mulattos in his fiction, is *not* determined by his blood and who successfully evades white people's definitions and demands.[22] Lucas takes on mythic characteristics; unlike other male characters, he is "impervious to time" (GDM 116). We are told that he "would not only outlive the present Edmonds as he had outlived the two preceding him, but would probably outlast the very ledgers which held the account" (GDM 117). The long quotation about his blood cited above affirms Lucas's timelessness: he is a "vessel" (a term otherwise reserved for women) rather than a "mausoleum," "durable" and "ancestryless" in the sense that he identifies completely with his grandfather McCaslin: "*He's more like old Carothers than all the rest of us put together, including old Carothers. He is both heir and prototype simultaneously . . . himself who fathered himself, intact and complete . . .*" (GDM 118). This is a language of transcendence in that it insists upon the simultaneity of past and present, the abolition of history as a linear phenomenon. One who is "both heir and prototype" has successfully defied history and achieved a degree of independence that is beyond the scope of time-entrapped characters, who are never free of the fetters of their personal and familial histories.

Several of Faulkner's old women, such as Jenny Du Pre and "Granny" Rosa Millard, are also depicted as unusually strong and independent figures. Faulkner can express this strength and even celebrate it for perhaps two basic reasons. First, the women are no longer sexual beings; that is, they are not experienced as sexual by the males who see them, so strength in them is not felt to be threatening in any way. Secondly, Faulkner is clearly perpetuating in these portrayals the highly romanticized Southern myth of its own past. However courageous such women actually were during the Civil War, the South went on to make of them legendary figures regularly outwitting the Yankees and preserving the way of life for which the South was fighting. Only in this golden past could women in Faulkner's fictive world safely be portrayed as being cleverer and braver than men. And it is characteristic of the myth itself that (1) they are so always in the absence of Southern men, and (2) that the people they dupe and dominate are Yankees, blacks, and children. But whenever women are not being manlike, brave in the way a man would be in the same circumstances, when they are acting "like women" (and, alas, there are only these two alternatives in Faulkner's fictive world), they evoke awe and bewilderment, as we shall soon see: "and he thought again how you could never really beat them because of their fluidity . . ." (ID 105).

Apart from such special figures, Faulkner occasionally depicts members of specific groups as approaching a way of being in the world that we might call timeless, if not precisely mythic. One such group includes characters who are indifferent to time because they exist apart from it—the retarded or mad characters, such as Benjy Compson, Darl Bundren, and Ike Snopes. Precisely because these characters' perceptions differ from the norm, they are put in their place and kept apart by the communities they frustrate. Darl's intuitive understanding of truths about his family (Dewey Dell's pregnancy, Jewel's paternity, their mother's death) is mystical, and as a result, his behavior comes to seem aberrant. He is sent eventually to the Jackson asylum, as is Benjy, who experiences past and present as apparently interchangeable impressions. Since he is not aware of the past *as* past, Benjy does not understand causation and is, in that regard, free of time. He lives out his life in rituals that perpetuate his sense of comfortableness in the world; driven around a statue in the "wrong" direction, he screams to recapture the ritualistic movement he counts on. Benjy's fierce clinging to ritual is an ironic instance of ritual that never did have meaning but that becomes all his life consists of. Ike Snopes is incapable of understanding spatial realities and unaware of temporal ones; he steps off into space because he cannot understand how to walk down stairs, and he holds on to the effigy of his beloved dead cow, not realizing any more than Benjy could the fact of his loss. We can hardly consider these figures to be mythic in the usual sense of the term, but it is clear that they are all somehow free of the fetters of time and space and that this freedom is a function of their mindlessness or madness. In Faulkner's world to have an intellect is to be caught endlessly in a troubling awareness of time and history.

Faulkner's portrayals of black people are relevant here as well. His characterizations differ considerably, depending upon whether he is describing them as individuals or as a group. Single characters are often well drawn, especially in the subtleties of their relationships with white people. Lucas's machinations involving his still and the divining machine in "The Fire and the Hearth" are comic and suggest masterfully the exasperation blacks and whites caused one another in such relationships. In "Pantaloon in Black" Faulkner exploits the narrow perceptions and understanding of white observers to show us the enormity with which black people are misunderstood by racists and to provide a wonderfully human portrait of Rider. When Faulkner muses about blacks as a group, however, his perceptions are quite different, and we find him attributing to black people the same unlikely characteristics he tends to give to women. Both are irrefutably Other, and the cluster of associations we saw in chapter 1 in the discussion of *Light in August* is evoked whenever white male characters ponder the nature of these two inscrutable groups. Thus, Gavin Stevens is able to say—bewilderingly—of women, "the past no more exists for them than morality does" (T 272). This sort of thinking—attributing particular qualities to blackness and femininity ipso facto—suggests the urgency of Faulkner's need to account imaginatively for the otherness of beings he does not understand. On occasion, he glosses over obvious sociological realities to pursue his imaginative vision of blacks as having achieved traits he finds appealing. He ignores the clear terror of a threatened lynching, for example, to describe the black people in a community as "just waiting, biding since theirs was an armament which the white man could not match nor—if he but knew it—even cope with: patience" (ID 96). Such conclusions are far from realistic; the best we can say of them is that they are consistent with Faulkner's mythic isolation of blacks and women as beings antithetical to himself and, thus, intrinsically mysterious.

There is another figure onto whom Faulkner projects a serene uninvolvement with the perceptions and responsibilities of men. In Faulkner's view, the mule is quintessentially indifferent to such concerns. Like women and blacks, the mule is portrayed as ineffably, mysteriously wise and self-sufficient. He is valued for having characteristics that suggest the feelings of inadequacy or frustration of his male observers. Quentin Compson watches a Negro on a mule at a train crossing and muses on "that quality about them of shabby and timeless patience, of static serenity: that blending of childlike and ready incompetence and paradoxical reliability that tends and protects them it loves out of all reason and robs them steadily and evades responsibility and obligations by means too barefaced to be called subterfuge even . . ." (TSAF 107–108). Like other protagonists, Quentin perceives mules—here, even identifying them with blacks—as protected by their nature from oppressive realities, from "responsibility and obligations." Although black people and mules obviously do have to work for others, the assumption implicit in Quentin's view of them is that they are independent and aloof, free from the constraints that matter to Faulkner's protagonists: time, ethical bounds, and so on. Their virtues—patience, serenity, "ready incompetence"—are the ones white males never achieve, are never allowed to achieve. Projected onto the mule are a strength of identity and an integrity that the Southern gentleman is always trying to attain: " . . . a mule is a gentleman too, and when you act courteous and respectful at him without trying to buy him or scare him, he'll act courteous and respectful back at you—as long as you dont overstep him. That's why you dont pet a mule like you do a horse: he knows you dont love him: you're just trying to fool him into doing something he already dont aim to do, and it insults him" (R 180).

Faulkner has chosen to apotheosize the mule, it seems, because it embodies genetically a transcendence of sexual distinctions; it represents an instance of miscegenation without horrible consequences—a sterile hybrid. The result of a crossing of apparently undeniable boundaries (those differentiating horses from asses), the mule emerges somehow as self-sufficient: "Father and mother he does not resemble, sons and daughters he will never have; vindictive and patient . . . solitary but without pride, self-sufficient but without vanity . . . Outcast and pariah, he has neither friend, wife, mistress nor sweetheart; celibate, he is unscarred, possesses neither pillar nor desert cave, he is not assaulted by temptations nor flagellated by dreams nor assuaged by visions . . . Misanthropic . . . meek . . . Ugly, untiring, and perverse . . ." (FD 314). The mule has achieved an aloofness that is associated with his freedom from sexuality ("neither pillar nor desert cave"). Not tormented by sexual attractions, the mule is free alike of the painfulness of longing and the encumbrance of relatives. He lives contentedly in the present; he is timeless: "free of the obligations of ancestry and the responsibilities of posterity, he has conquered not only life but death too and hence is immortal . . . incorrigible . . . still free, still coping" (R 92).

In his wistful mythology of the mule, Faulkner accomplishes an imaginative fusion of differences[23] that ends in an autonomy impossible among his mulatto figures (the words share etymological roots), an autonomy that is openly longed for by his protagonists, who are entangled with women and time and, thus, unfree.[24]

Women themselves, when they are felt to be sexual beings, evoke in Faulkner's males, as they appear to have done in Faulkner himself, a profound and powerful ambivalence. On the one hand, Faulkner was deeply romantic and tended to create highly idealized versions of his relationships with the women he loved. David Minter's discussion of these relationships reveals that, like some of his early protagonists, Faulkner may have tended to "[cultivate] passion in order to sublimate it."[25] He appears to have struggled through much of his life with the "dilemma of desire,"[26] the realization that when we get what we desire, we lose it. It never retains the "bright shape" it took in our minds when it *was* desire and not yet attainment; inevitably it disappoints. This romantic desire for precisely what cannot be is something Faulkner appears to have shared with Quentin Compson in his love for Caddy; Faulkner and Quentin both speak of incest—Faulkner, metaphorically—"as a way of transmuting perishable love into enduring bond."[27] Faulkner seems always to have idealized the women he loved, to have feared the end of the romantic illusion. It seems significant that in Joan Williams's *The Wintering*, a novel based on her relationship with Faulkner, she should characterize the protagonist Jeff Almoner as loving knowing "that he is fated to lose the girl-woman, daughter-lover named Amy Howard—that in the end 'the face and figure' locked away in his mind will be all that is left him." [28] In a letter to Meta Carpenter, Faulkner wrote that "grief is the inevictable part of it, the thing that makes it cohere; that grief is the only thing you are capable of sustaining, keeping; that what is valuable is what you have lost, since then you never had the chance to wear out and so lose it shabbily." [29]

The other side of this powerful longing for romantic passion is an equally deep distrust and bitterness toward women. Minter correlates this basic dis-ease with Faulkner's continual movement between participation in and detachment from life: Faulkner "feared nothing more deeply than the artist's reluctance to brave 'chance and circumstance.' A part of him had long fought all signs of surrender to such fear, particularly as it manifested itself in fear of women." [30] It is, of course, this side of the ambivalence that is more often manifested in Faulkner's prose. He projects his uneasiness, his fear of engulfment, and his disgust (woman as "physical spittoon") [31] onto his fictional characters, letting them act out their extraordinary anxiety in the presence of feminine sexuality. As a consequence, Faulkner's female characters tend to be distorted or mythicized beings, the projection of a masculine consciousness at its most vulnerable. The consciousness that informs Faulkner's prose attributes to women the very strengths that he, a white Southern gentleman, feels to be the counterparts to his own weaknesses: the woman is serene, he is tormented (we think of Lena Grove and Eula Varner on the one hand, Joe Christmas and Gavin Stevens on the other); she is rarely cerebral or articulate, he is often both, and he suffers from a brooding nostalgia; she is rich, fecund, enveloping, he is threatened by those qualities. [32] She can encounter and survive realities that leave men enervated. In "Carcassonne" Faulkner writes that women "have learned how to live unconfused by reality, impervious to it" (CS 898). Being "other," woman is said to be able to deal with the things that feel most alien to men—the unknown (her "knowledge" does not need to be learned) and death: "It's not men who cope with death; they resist, try to fight back and get their brains trampled out in consequence; where

women just flank it, envelop it in one soft and instantaneous con-
federation of unresistance like cotton batting or cobwebs, already
de-stingered and harmless, not merely reduced to size and usable
but even useful like a penniless bachelor or spinster connection always available to fill an empty space or conduct an extra guest
down to dinner" (R 38).

Faulkner's male characters tend to perceive women as containing spaces, places that (1) when benevolent, offer serenity, security,
and peace and (2) when threatening—that is, sexual—seem capable of devouring the man who gets too close. Men's sisters, like
Narcissa Benbow and Caddy Compson, are likened to pools of
water near which their brothers hover like insects or birds or in
which they long to rest as swimmers. Women with whom the men
in the novels are actively sexual are also ponds and seas, but their
manifest eroticism makes them dangerous. Of Belle Mitchell, who
becomes his lover, Horace Benbow thinks, "And then Belle again,
enveloping him like a rich and fatal drug, like a motionless and
cloying sea in which he watched himself drown" (FD 285). The
imagery of destruction is omnipresent: whenever a sexual woman is
experienced at close range, Faulkner's male characters start perceiving things in terms of annihilation, entrapment, engulfment,
and corruption. Quentin's father says of them: "Delicate equilibrium of periodical filth. . . . with all that inside of them shapes
an outward suavity waiting for a touch to. Liquid putrefaction like
drowned things floating like pale rubber flabbily filled getting the
odour of honeysuckle all mixed up" (TSAF 159). Faulkner associates the physicality of women with corruption, with his own bodily
consciousness of "that steady decay which had set up within his
body on the day of his birth" (CS 896–897)[33]—much as Joe Christmas had confused the two.

There is a fascinating biographical counterpart to these fictional associations. Minter tells us that Faulkner came to see the
growth of a girl through puberty into sexuality as virtually a re-
enactment of the Fall.[34] He thought of his daughter Jill's incipient
womanhood as the end of something precious, and he began to
choose as lovers women young enough to be "girl-children" to
him.[35] With Meta Carpenter, Faulkner felt a deep fascination that
involved both the excitement of illicit sex and a transcendent romantic passion. He coped with the hesitation born of his guilt and
his passion by creating two imaginative versions of Meta as his

lover, one idealized, the other eroticized. He turned her into a "girl-child" by seeing her and referring to her at times as far younger than she was. In the language of chapter 1, Faulkner split Meta imaginatively into two figures who embodied ambiguities within himself. As Minter explains, "If on one side these revisions reduced Faulkner's fear of being engulfed, on another they reduced his fear of being contaminated. For he was taking his lover back not only to a time when she was sweet and timid but also to a time before the onset of 'periodical filth.' . . . Through removals and dissociations, Faulkner attempted to move Meta toward conjunction with an acceptably pure shape—that of a young girl."[36] Since he was indeed an ardent and attentive, if cautious, lover, we might conclude that this imaginative shaping of his relationship with Meta Carpenter was anticipated by the imaginative shapings we discern in his fiction when male protagonists attempt to cope with the anxiety of closeness to women. What we don't see in the fiction is a viable picture of romantic love; *The Wild Palms*, as I have suggested elsewhere, is a failure in this regard, for the classically anal compulsive imagery pervading the story systematically undermines the rather continual talk of romantic transcendence.[37] It seems likely that Faulkner's writing focused on issues that caused him anxiety, in a sense freeing him to seek out the love that, despite his protestations of independence, he needed. One hopes that the fiction freed him to some degree to find in the love relationships the very qualities missing in his fictional male-female encounters: joy, playfulness, fulfillment. But an underlying uneasiness is still evident: in spite of his love for Meta Carpenter, he avoided living with her.

Most of Faulkner's fictive women tend to be parodies: sexually intense physical presences, desiccating spinsters, faded housewives, or venerated old ladies. When he does attempt to draw a fully rounded, strong female character, he can conceive of strength only in masculine terms. Several women, for example, are approachable as sexual figures because they have recognizably masculine features or outlooks. Harry Wilbourne sees Charlotte Rittenmeyer in *The Wild Palms* as being "*not only a better man and a better gentleman than I am, she is a better everything than I will ever be*" (WP 207). He lets her be "the man" in the relationship: she defines the meaning of their love; she initiates their lovemaking. Nevertheless, for Harry, sharing sex with her means total helplessness: " . . . the terror in which you surrender volition, hope, all—the darkness, the falling, the thunder of solitude, the shock, the death, the moment when, stopped physically by the ponderable clay, you yet feel all your life rush out of you into the pervading immemorial blind receptive matrix, the hot fluid blind foundation—grave-womb or womb-grave, it's all one" (WP 138).[38]

Addie Bundren in *As I Lay Dying* is masculine in many ways as well. Despite her elaborate disclaimer that words are meaningless entities, empty shapes that men often substitute for genuine experiences, Addie shows us in the obsessive quality of her monologue her own reliance on words to justify her behavior and her need for revenge ("my revenge would be that he would never know I was taking revenge," AILD 164), and her measuring of things to get them even again (the babies she "gives" Anse to replace those she feels she has robbed him of): all of her habits of mind and perception, in other words, are symptomatic of masculine ways of being in the world in Faulkner's fiction. Joanna Burden and Bobbie Allen, too, as we saw in chapter 1, are approachable because they appear to be masculine, for sight (delusively) assures Joe Christmas that they are not likely to destroy him.

The quality that links women in Faulkner's stories to blacks, to the wilderness, to the special, serene figures he creates, and to mules is their ability—in the eyes always of the male observer—to live contentedly in the present moment, simply to wait, not to struggle with the fact of time. Projecting this characteristic onto beings who feel alien to him, the Faulknerian protagonist then responds in awe and despair and envy to creatures whom he sees as living without the tortured self-awareness that dominates his consciousness. It is precisely when Faulkner attempts to portray characters whom he sees as finding a degree of peace living in the present moment that his characterizations become mythic. The figures are in one real sense stereotypes in that they are assumed to have various characteristics simply by virtue of belonging to a particular category of people. They represent a failure in realistic characterization in that Faulkner never—in his fiction, at least—overcomes his assumption that they share mysterious qualities forever denied his protagonists. They represent projections implicit in the perceptions of the Southern white male protagonists, so they exist more for the sake of what they represent to those characters than in their own right.

The ambivalence that we find in Faulkner's fictive presentations of women characters seems a basic component of the perceptual habits this study has attempted to elucidate. The consciousness through which perceptions are controlled in his stories is an uneasy one, caught between the conflicting desires to participate fully in life and to withdraw into isolation, to experience flux and to deny it by exerting control. It is a tension that Faulkner felt strongly in his own life, in part because of his desire to be an artist. Minter emphasizes this tension throughout his biography of Faulkner, who both "needed to feel that he was a man of action" and yet was drawn into silence as an observer and recorder of the life around him. Especially early in his career, he felt "deep ambivalence toward the role of the observer and the fate it [implied] . . . the persona of *The Marble Faun*, for example, describes itself as 'mute and impotent.'" [39]

A woman Faulkner loved as a young man appears to have intuited the severity of this conflict in him. As Minter writes, "Helen Baird seems almost to have recognized . . . that [Faulkner] stood outside the life he lived, jotting things down as he went along; that there was a doubleness in his emotional entanglements; that he deliberately cultivated emotions with the intention of transmuting them; and that he found her more compelling because he knew her to be unattainable." [40] She may have refused to become involved with a man she knew would continually resist closeness. Soon thereafter, when Faulkner married Estelle Franklin, she quickly discovered the degree to which he insisted on isolation, and her sense of abandonment for a time left her suicidal. [41]

We cannot know the precise etiology of Faulkner's ambivalence toward life and toward women, in particular, but we do know some of its consequences. Early in his life, he began to withdraw into periods of silence, into stoicism, into observation of events around him. His relationships, as Minter documents, were highly stylized throughout his life. He appears to have been a deeply disappointed romantic, who associated great love, great heroism, and great art all "under the aspect of the unattainable." [42] We know some of his disappointments: Estelle's first marriage to another man, his being too small to serve as a pilot in World War I and too old for World War II (leaving him feeling cheated of a chance to duplicate his great-grandfather's courage), the early reception of his poetry and stories. But the stories and novels tell us of still

deeper loss. On numerous occasions he makes his characters orphans or children who have been severely let down by their parents. Sometimes the parental generation is simply omitted.[43] In
two early short stories featuring the Compson children, Faulkner
"poised [them] at the end of childhood and the beginning of awareness—a moment that possessed particular poignancy for him. . . .
In 'A Justice,' as twilight descends around them and their world
begins to fade, loss, consternation, and bafflement become almost
all they know."[44] It is true, as Minter writes, that these stories and
The Sound and the Fury were written at a time when Faulkner's personal and professional lives were in crisis, but nevertheless I think
it noteworthy that he locates such suffering precisely at the point
where childhood illusions must be given up. Faulkner himself had
grown up on stories of the adventures and glory of his ancestors; he
must simultaneously have been realizing that those times had irrevocably faded, that he would not be able to create that sense of
himself as a man of action, an aristocrat, and a hero that he had
imagined. He symbolically embraced a far more appealing past,
first by changing the spelling of his own name (adding the "u" to
Falkner) and, later, in spelling his great-grandfather's name with a
"u" as well.

In terms of his relationships with women, Faulkner's idealization of them seems to converge with many of his concerns as an
artist. In early work, such as the Elmer stories, Faulkner depicts
the artist as attempting to recreate some "vague shape" in his imagination, something representing, as Minter expresses it, "the core
for him of everything he dreads and desires."[45] The perfection of
this inner shape (in which beauty, desire, and passion seem one)
means that any actual work of art or act of heroism or love will only
approximate the original passionate conception. This is the "dilemma of desire" mentioned earlier. To have something is to become inevitably aware of its limitations, the ways in which it is not
equal to the passion in which it began. Thus, Faulkner's disappointments, his sense of loss, led him into an idealization of things
which cannot be and which, therefore, cannot fade. Caddy Compson is the apotheosis of the images that Faulkner brought together
in speaking of his art. She is unattainable, being both "the sister he
never had and . . . the daughter he was fated to lose."[46] Because
her portrayal is done only obliquely, she can retain the imaginative
shape Faulkner is reaching toward. She is his "heart's darling."[47]

Minter writes: "In a figure like Caddy Compson he had brought many of his loves together. Creating for 'himself a maid that life had not had time to create,' he had 'laid upon her frail and unbowed shoulders the whole burden of man's history of his impossible heart's desire.'"[48]

Caddy, in turn, is linked to an image we noted earlier, the vase or urn, an image for Faulkner of the work of art. Minter writes: "the vase becomes both Caddy and *The Sound and the Fury*; both 'the beautiful one' for whom he created the novel as a commodious space and the novel in which she found protection and privacy as well as expression. In its basic doubleness the vase is many things: a haven or shelter into which the artist may retreat; a feminine ideal to which he can give his devotion; a work of art that he can leave behind when he is dead; and a burial urn that will contain at least one expression of his self as an artist. If it is a mouth he may freely kiss, it is also a world in which he may find shelter . . ."[49] Minter recognizes the overdetermined quality of this favorite Faulknerian image; in the language of my own study, he has seen the vase as a container in which precious things may be preserved, a place in which he can rest and be safe, a womblike place, and a trace of himself as an artist. The urn, the object of art, the novel in which she appears, and Caddy herself all become associated with the bright shape that is their source: "it takes only one book to do it. It's not the sum of a lot of scribbling, it's one perfect book, you see. It's one single urn or shape that you want to do."[50]

In his art, then, Faulkner makes a choice very like that of his protagonists who feel incestuous longings for their sisters. It is precisely their unattainability that constitutes their value. Forbidden love is desirable because it will survive as passion, not end in decay or disappointment or shabbiness.[51] Faulkner associated his "heart's darling" Caddy "with Keats's urn, which he in turn associated with life and with art—with life because it depicted love that was dreamed yet denied, felt yet deferred; and with art because it epitomized form."[52] To feel something yet defer it is to sustain passion and not risk loss. It is also a masterful solution to an ambivalence toward physical closeness with the object of your love.

Faulkner had suggested in the Elmer stories that works of art and women are "substitutes for, signs of, the impossible and forbidden shape" in the artist's mind.[53] If he continued to believe this about art—and his deep depressions after each novel was completed suggest that he did—then his conception of art implicitly entailed a struggle to evoke something essentially ineffable. It entailed as well a continual sense of having failed, as Walter Slatoff acknowledged in entitling his book on Faulkner *Quest for Failure*. In reaching toward his subject, Faulkner structured his quest uniquely by presenting his characters' perceptions in ways allowing them an illusion of control. If life denied Faulkner precisely this sense of mastery, his defenses, as Minter suggests, consisted of withdrawing into silence and observation, stylizing his relationships with others, idealizing his artistic goals and his passions, and writing his extraordinary stories. He appears to have felt in his life and to have perpetuated in his theory of the meaning of art an ongoing sense of loss. Fictionally that sense of loss is expressed in the wide variety of narrative strategies we have considered. Perhaps any writer's work is in some sense a response to the loss or absence of something, but surely the configuration of strategies, images, and themes explored here is evidence of a uniquely Faulknerian confrontation of his longing for "*that might-have-been which is the single rock we cling to above the maelstrom of unbearable reality*" (AA 149–150).

Notes

Introduction

1. In addition to those cited elsewhere in this introduction, the following works are especially helpful: Arnold H. Modell, M.D., *Object Love and Reality: An Introduction to a Psychoanalytic Theory of Object Relations* (New York: International Universities Press, Inc., 1968); D. W. Winnicott, "The Location of Cultural Experience," *International Journal of Psychoanalysis* 48 (1967): 368–372; Marion Milner, "Aspects of Symbolism in Comprehension of the Not-Self," *International Journal of Psychoanalysis* 33 (1952): 181–195.

2. This paragraph and the next are heavily indebted to D. W. Winnicott, "Transitional Objects and Transitional Phenomena," *International Journal of Psychoanalysis* 34 (1953): 89–97.

3. As David Bleich has written, "By naming the absent object, the infant predicates it on its previous presence: 'Mommy gone.'" "New Considerations of the Infantile Acquisition of Language and Symbolic Thought," *Psychoanalytic Review* 63 (1976): 56.

4. See Michael Balint, *The Basic Fault: Therapeutic Aspects of Regression* (London: Tavistock Publications, 1968), especially pp. 64–72, for a discussion of the consequences of such rigid responses to the trauma of separation.

5. Heinz Lichtenstein, "Identity and Sexuality: A Study of Their Interrelationship in Man," *Journal of the American Psychoanalytic Association* 9 (1961): 208.

6. André Bleikasten has made this same observation: "What [*The Sound and the Fury*] is about is loss: loss of love through loss of self, loss of self through loss of love." *The Most Splendid Failure: Faulkner's "The Sound and the Fury"* (Bloomington: Indiana University Press, 1976), p. 173.

7. John T. Irwin, *Doubling and Incest/Repetition and Revenge: A Speculative Reading of Faulkner* (Baltimore: Johns Hopkins University Press, 1975), p. 7.

8. David L. Minter, *William Faulkner: His Life and Work* (Baltimore: Johns Hopkins University Press, 1980), p. 78.

9. Ibid., p. 77.

10. Ibid., p. xii.
11. Ibid., p. 131.

1. Identity and the Spatial Imagination

1. Frederick L. Gwynn and Joseph L. Blotner, eds., *Faulkner in the University: Class Conferences at the University of Virginia 1957–58* (Charlottesville: University of Virginia Press, 1959), p. 72.

2. Lichtenstein, "Identity and Sexuality," p. 189: "Psychoanalytic evidence makes it . . . probable that the maintenance of identity in man has priority over any other principle determining human behavior, not only the reality principle but also the pleasure principle."

3. The term is Alfred Kazin's in "Faulkner: The Rhetoric and the Agony," *Virginia Quarterly Review* 18 (1942): 390–391.

4. Leslie Fiedler has argued persuasively that such identity problems lead to an ambivalence that appears to permeate American literature, not merely the literature of the South. See especially *Love and Death in the American Novel* (New York: Dell, 1966).

5. David Minter notes that many of Faulkner's characters are depicted as betrayed children with inadequate, inaccessible, or too demanding parents. Minter, *Faulkner*, pp. 18, 87, 104, 119, 154. Faulkner appears to have been disappointed in his own father and to have embraced the romantic image of his great-grandfather instead. Of his relationship to his mother, his friend Phil Stone said "that all the Falkner boys were tied to their mother and resented it" and that this was "probably partly responsible . . . for an animosity toward women that he saw in Bill." Joseph Blotner, *Faulkner: A Biography*, vol. 1 (New York: Random House, 1974), p. 631.

6. Blotner, *Faulkner*, vol. 1, pp. 76–78 ff.

7. Minter, *Faulkner*, p. 93.

8. Ibid., p. 17.

9. Ibid., p. xi.

10. Ibid., p. 17.

11. Minter writes that Faulkner "built a life that he permitted others to enter, so far as possible, only on his own terms. He wanted to be independent—to be a 'proud and self-sufficient beast,' one who 'walked by himself, needing nothing from anyone, or at least never letting them know it.'" Minter, *Faulkner*, p. 116. Faulkner's words are from a letter to Joan Williams, November 6, 1952, William Faulkner Collections, Alderman Library, University of Virginia, Charlottesville; quoted also in Blotner, *Faulkner*, vol. 2, p. 1437.

12. Minter notes preoccupations that Doc Hines, Mr. McEachern, and Percy Grimm have in common in *Light in August*: "Filth and abom-

ination provide the categories in terms of which they understand most of life, including everyone who is either female or black." *Faulkner*, p. 132.

13. Blotner, *Faulkner*, vol. 1, p. 498.

14. Faulkner himself often reifies these words by capitalizing them.

15. Phyllis Greenacre, "Early Physical Determinants in the Development of the Sense of Identity," *Journal of the American Psychoanalytic Association* 6 (1958): 613–614.

16. The fact of this relationship is almost a commonplace in Faulkner criticism. Just a few of the articles reflecting aspects of Lena's significance include Robert W. Kirk, "Faulkner's Lena Grove," *Georgia Review* 21 (1967): 57–64; Norman Holmes Pearson, "Lena Grove," *Shenandoah* 3 (1952): 3–7; David L. Minter, introduction to *Twentieth Century Interpretations of Light in August* (Englewood Cliffs, N.J.: Prentice-Hall, 1969), pp. 1–16; and Cleanth Brooks, introduction to *Light in August*, by William Faulkner (New York: Random House, Modern Library, 1968), pp. v–xxv.

17. Richard P. Adams writes: "In many passages of Faulkner's fiction, eating and breathing are equivalent to living, whereas the feeling of suffocation or a refusal of food, and especially the act of vomiting, suggest an inability to live or a rejection of life." *Faulkner: Myth and Motion* (Princeton: Princeton University Press, 1968), p. 125.

18. I am thinking of such figures as Quentin Compson, Henry Sutpen, Bayard Sartoris, Horace Benbow, and even to some degree Flem Snopes.

19. Among critics who have discussed the symbolism of the circle in this novel are Richard Chase, "The Stone and the Crucifixion: Faulkner's *Light in August*," *Kenyon Review* 10 (1948): 539–551; and James L. Roberts, "The Individual and the Community: Faulkner's *Light in August*," in *Studies in American Literature*, edited by Waldo McNeir and Leo B. Levy (Baton Rouge: Louisiana State University Press, 1960), pp. 132–153.

20. The nature of this entrapment will become clearer as we explore Faulkner's use of space and objects as containers, sometimes benevolent, sometimes threatening. Those that imply confinement, as do circles, patterns, and the cage mentioned in the epigraph to this chapter, are the latter type.

21. Richard Adams sees the tension between motion and stasis as a basic element in Faulkner's stories; he describes Lena as "pure motion, tranquilly natural, comfortable, and inevitable, completely in harmony with the motion of life in the earth." *Myth and Motion*, p. 86.

22. Heinz Lichtenstein suggests that certain aspects of sadomasochistic behavior may be accounted for by a fundamental feeling of self-negation, in other words, by an absence of the kinds of responses from

other people that normally lead to a sense of personal well-being. In his view, such an existentially insecure person may be led into the types of behavior we find in Joe Christmas. See "The Malignant No: A Hypothesis Concerning the Interdependence of the Sense of Self and the Instinctual Drives," in *The Unconscious Today: Essays in Honor of Max Schur*, edited by Mark Kanzer (New York: International Universities Press, 1971), pp. 147–176.

23. Sadistic behavior can serve the same psychic functions as masochism. Compare Joe's behavior with Addie Bundren's recollection of her treatment of her students: "I would look forward to the times when they faulted, so I could whip them. When the switch fell I could feel it upon my flesh; when it welted and ridged it was my blood that ran, and I would think with each blow of the switch: *Now you are aware of me!* Now I am something in your secret and selfish life, who have marked your blood with my own for ever and ever" (AILD 162, emphasis mine).

24. McEachern's Calvinistic mind sees the world in terms of discrete situations, each of which has its appropriate and necessary rule of behavior. The clarity of these directives—"thou shalt" or "thou shalt not"—makes Calvinism very appealing to someone like Joe, who often resembles McEachern later in his life and who consistently feels betrayed when people (nearly always women) do not follow the rules that he has decided to apply to a situation.

25. In *Flags in the Dust* Horace Benbow is obsessed with a vase/urn that he equates with his sister Narcissa, calls by her name, and keeps by his bedside. The novel is filled with allusions to John Keats's "Ode on a Grecian Urn."

26. These beatings—in their rhythmic, nearly emotionless deliberation—also reveal Joe's identification with McEachern, the only person who has been a figure of strength to him.

27. See R. D. Laing, *Self and Others* (Harmondsworth, England: Penguin Books Ltd., 1961), pp. 86–87 and his chapters "False and Untenable Positions" and "Attributions and Injunctions."

28. Carl G. Jung, ed., *Man and His Symbols* (Garden City: Doubleday, 1964); see especially chapter 3, "The Process of Individuation," by M.-L. von Franz, which discusses the anima and animus as aspects of the psyche.

29. Faulkner's own writing took on a ritualistic tone in the repetitiveness of his return to the same themes and stories.

30. See R. D. Laing, *The Divided Self: An Existential Study in Sanity and Madness* (Harmondsworth, England: Penguin Books Ltd., 1960), especially chapters 5, 6, and 7 on the nature of inner and false selves.

31. "This double orientation of the term identity appears to be a special aspect of the fact that the concept of identity can be perceived

only as relative to its opposite, the idea of change. . . . Life, as a biological as well as mental phenomenon, can be defined as identity in change." Lichtenstein, "Identity and Sexuality," p. 188.

32. The terms "pass" (to pass as a white person, for example) and "cross over" are obvious, explicit references to the presence of boundaries, as are many of the verbs that describe racial and sexual interactions. Faulkner's drawings as a young man, incidentally, use checkerboard squares repeatedly in the apparel of harlequin figures, on floors, and as backdrops. See Blotner, *Faulkner*, vol. 1, pp. 208 and 273.

Finally, here is V. K. Ratliff's narration of Gavin Stevens musing about football: "him talking about how the game of football could be brought up to date in keeping with the progress of the times by giving ever body a football too so ever body would be in the game; or maybe better still, keep jest one football but *abolish the boundaries* so that a smart feller for instance could hide the ball under his shirttail and slip off into the bushes and circle around town and come in through a back alley and cross the goal before anybody even missed he was gone" (M 149, emphasis mine).

33. Even informally Faulkner would sometimes objectify aspects of himself as if they were acting in opposition to him. In an article in the *New Yorker*, Faulkner was described as he worked in Saxe Commins's office at Random House, interrupting his typing to say, "Ah wish mah doom would lift or come on. Ah got work to do." James B. Meriwether and Michael Millgate, eds., *Lion in the Garden: Interviews with William Faulkner 1926–62* (New York: Random House, 1968), p. 76.

34. Malcolm Cowley, *The Faulkner-Cowley File: Letters and Memories, 1944–1962* (London: Chatto & Windus, 1966), pp. 90 and 89.

35. See Bleikasten, *Most Splendid Failure*, p. 127. There is a temporal as well as a spatial "difference" which boundaries and definitions serve to locate. The temporal aspects of this descriptive problem are considered in the next chapter.

36. Faulkner's *Absalom, Absalom!*, another by no means isolated case, is pervaded with references to a dual vision. It begins with "two separate Quentins now—the Quentin Compson preparing for Harvard . . . and the Quentin Compson who was still too young to deserve yet to be a ghost, but nevertheless having to be one for all that, since he was born and bred in the deep South . . ." (AA 9); and it ends with a fusion of the two young men in Cambridge with two young men decades earlier whose story they are imaginatively recreating: "now it was not two but four of them riding the two horses through the dark over the frozen December ruts of that Christmas Eve: four of them and then just two— Charles-Shreve and Quentin-Henry . . ." (AA 334; see also AA 303).

37. See Darrel Abel, "Frozen Movement in *Light in August*," *Boston*

University Studies in English 3 (1957): 32–44; Alfred Kazin, "The Stillness of *Light in August*," *Partisan Review* 24 (1957): 519–538; V. S. Pritchett, "Time Frozen," *Partisan Review* 21 (1954): 557–561; and Karl E. Zink, "Flux and the Frozen Moment: The Imagery of Stasis in Faulkner's Prose," *PMLA* 71 (1956): 285–301.

38. On several occasions Joseph Blotner points out Faulkner's liking for this descriptive technique, especially dominant in his early writing. For example, in 1922 Faulkner reviewed Joseph Hergesheimer's novel *Linda Condon*, declaring "that it was not really a novel but 'more like a lovely Byzantine frieze: a few unforgettable figures in silent arrested motion, forever beyond the reach of time and troubling the heart like music.'" *Faulkner*, vol. 1, p. 343; see also pp. 395 and 516. Blotner is quoting from Faulkner's "Books and Things: Joseph Hergesheimer," reprinted in *William Faulkner: Early Prose and Poetry*, edited by Carvel Collins (London: Jonathan Cape, 1963), p. 101.

39. One of these artifacts, the river, is discussed in the next chapter. Discussions of Faulkner's use of landscape are generally dispersed through essays focusing on other matters, but see William Van O'Connor, "The Wilderness Theme in Faulkner's 'The Bear,'" *Accent* 13 (1953): 12–20; and François L. Pitavy, "The Landscape in *Light in August*," *Mississippi Quarterly* 23 (1970): 265–272.

40. See Jean-Paul Sartre, "Time in Faulkner: *The Sound and the Fury*," translated by Martine Darmon, in *William Faulkner: Three Decades of Criticism*, edited by Frederick Hoffman and Olga W. Vickery (East Lansing: Michigan State University Press, 1960), pp. 225–232.

41. Walter J. Ong, S.J., *The Presence of the Word* (New York: Simon and Schuster, 1970), pp. 95–101.

42. Quoted in Blotner, *Faulkner*, vol. 2, pp. 1105–1106. Minter emphasizes Faulkner's ambivalence toward the external world and its demands and his rather continual movement back and forth between participation and withdrawal: "Toward his world, he remained deeply ambivalent: drawn to it, he could half enter it; offended by it, he became uneasy and pulled back." Minter, *Faulkner*, p. 75. Minter believes that Faulkner jumped horses and took risks in part to achieve a sense of mastery and in part because facing danger may have been "the only way he had of showing contempt for destruction" (p. 245).

43. "Faulkner had been undergoing the accumulation of problems, frustrations, and anxieties that had sent him into collapses in Hollywood. Sometimes [his daughter] Jill could see one coming when, a few days before the onset, he would begin to recite 'The Phoenix and the Turtle' . . . She pleaded with him to hold on, to resist. 'Think of me,' she appealed. But it was already too late." Blotner, *Faulkner*, vol. 2, p. 1204; see also pp. 1160 and 1162.

44. See Minter, *Faulkner*, pp. 16, 105, 133.

45. *The Complete Works of Shakespeare*, 3rd ed., edited by David Bevington (Glenview, Ill.: Scott, Foresman and Company, 1980), pp. 1573–1574.

46. Quoted in Blotner, *Faulkner*, vol. 1, pp. 531–532.

2. Precarious Coherence: Objects through Time

1. See Peter Swiggart, "Time in Faulkner's Novels," *Modern Fiction Studies* 1 (1955): 25–29; Abel, "Frozen Movement in *Light in August*," pp. 32–44; Margaret Church, "William Faulkner: Myth and Duration," *Time and Reality: Studies in Contemporary Fiction* (Chapel Hill: University of North Carolina Press, 1963), pp. 227–250; Donald M. Kartiganer, "*The Sound and the Fury* and Faulkner's Quest for Form," *ELH* 37 (1970): 613–639; Shirley P. Callen, "Bergsonian Dynamism in the Writings of William Faulkner," Ph.D. diss., Tulane University, 1963.

2. As Bergson explains, survival that is simply stasis or passivity is quite different from the ongoing growth characteristic of duration: "For an ego which does not change does not *endure*, and a psychic state which remains the same so long as it is not replaced by the following state does not *endure* either." Henri Bergson, *Creative Evolution*, translated by Arthur Mitchell (New York: Random House, Modern Library, 1944), p. 6. The endurance of Dilsey and others like her is a changing that evolves with the emerging demands of her environment; her perspective enlarges with new experiences: "I seed de beginnin, en now I sees de endin" (TSAF 371).

Faulkner was enthusiastic about *Creative Evolution*. Husserl and others have since modified many of Bergson's observations, as, for example, in their elucidation of the role of intentionality in perception. My concern here and in the following chapter is not to defend the precision of Bergson's insights but rather to show their value in illuminating the vision we actually discern in Faulkner's prose.

3. Bergson, *Creative Evolution*, p. 297.

4. Ibid., p. 4.

5. Ibid., p. 6.

6. See Adams, *Myth and Motion*, p. 13: "by Faulkner's logic, the only way to be motionless is to be dead." Adams argues, too, that "motion cannot be directly described" and that the means an artist must necessarily use in trying to describe it are "artificial" (p. 5).

7. Bergson, *Creative Evolution*, p. 296. See Adams, *Myth and Motion*, pp. 110–111.

8. The danger of boundary loss and, moreover, the association of women and their qualities with the earth (fecundity, for example) that I

posited in chapter 1 are vividly presented in a passage about the dangers of being pulled in by the earth (M 402) discussed in chapter 4.

9. Once we are aware of Faulkner's tendency to set objects firmly against their backgrounds, the peculiar vividness of a number of his descriptions is accounted for. For example, when he speaks of land, trees, or other natural things that have been violated by man, he regularly uses images of scars and healing to suggest nature's impulse to undo the effects of human presence: "an old field . . . its plow-scars long healed over" (FD 355); "The lane . . . became . . . a mere path scarred quietly into new grass" (TSAF 165). This image suggests the tendency of matter to flow back into simpler states, but it also emphasizes that scars are especially obvious phenomena that can only be known by virtue of their background, what it is that they are scarring. Elsewhere, characters' eyes are described as pieces of coal pressed into dough, and old Bayard Sartoris sits dressed "in immaculate linen and a geranium like a merry wound" (FD 244). The juxtaposition of the thing being described and its background creates a contrast that *is* the vividness of the image.

The technique of setting things against their background or context in order to make them vivid and that of setting things in opposition to one another (blackness/whiteness, etc.) that we looked at in the last chapter seem fused in the following passage, in which Faulkner makes the definitions of "sanity" and "madness" interdependent: "*as if he had reached for the moment some interval of sanity such as the mad know, just as the sane have intervals of madness to keep them aware that they are sane*" (AA 165).

10. See also John K. Simon, "The Scene and the Imagery of Metamorphosis in *As I Lay Dying*," *Criticism* 7 (1965): 1–22; and Rosemary Franklin, "Animal Magnetism in *As I Lay Dying*," *American Quarterly* 18 (1966): 24–34.

11. See also Arthur L. Ford, "Dust and Dreams: A Study of Faulkner's 'Dry September,'" *College English* 24 (1962): 219–220; and Ralph H. Wolfe and Edgar F. Daniels, "Beneath the Dust of 'Dry September,'" *Studies in Short Fiction* 1 (1964): 158–159.

12. Consider Nancy's fate in "That Evening Sun"; Emily Grierson and Homer Barron's relationship and Homer's death in "A Rose for Emily"; *The Sound and the Fury*, which Faulkner repeatedly affirmed is about Caddy and in which she alone has no voice; the murder of Joanna Burden in *Light in August*; and almost everything about the Sutpens in *Absalom, Absalom!*

André Bleikasten considers Caddy a "pure figure of *absence*" and argues that as early as *Soldiers' Pay*, Faulkner had established a pattern "to be reused in a number of later works: some fading figure—a shadowy presence or a haunting absence rather than a fully realized character in the usual sense—becomes the static center which sets everything in motion, and around which all the other characters revolve in concentric circles, each of them responding to it in his own personal way." *Most Splendid Failure*, p. 56 and pp. 19–20.

13. Roma King, Jr., "The Janus Symbol in *As I Lay Dying*," *University of Kansas City Review* 21 (1955): 289.

14. Flem wears a black felt banker's hat for three years, apparently never taking it off, but it "still looked new. No, it didn't look like it belonged to anybody, even after day and night for three years, not even sweated . . ." (M 65).

15. Several critics have recognized one or more of these configurations. See especially Bleikasten, *Most Splendid Failure*, p. 134, and Judith Slater's suggestive essay, "Quentin's Tunnel Vision: Modes of Perception and Their Stylistic Realization in *The Sound and the Fury*," *Literature and Psychology* 27 (1977): 4–15.

16. This motivation for Quentin's behavior is explored at length in Irwin's provocative study, *Doubling and Incest/Repetition and Revenge*; see also Bleikasten, *Most Splendid Failure*, p. 136.

17. Quentin's father sees women as "shapes," and in *The Sound and the Fury*, as in *Light in August*, they are described in terms revealing a masculine disgust with the mysteries, rhythms, and processes that tie woman so closely to nature. Consistent with that bifurcation of qualities that we considered in the last chapter, man is characterized as dust and woman as liquid. She is flowing, insidious, threatening: "Because women so delicate so mysterious Father said. Delicate equilibrium of periodical filth between two moons balanced. Moons he said full and yellow as harvest moons her hips thighs. Outside outside of them always but. Yellow. Feet soles with walking like. Then know that some man that all those mysterious and imperious concealed. With all that inside of them shapes an outward suavity waiting for a touch to. Liquid putrefaction like drowned things floating like pale rubber flabbily filled getting the odour of honeysuckle all mixed up" (TSAF 159).

18. See Bleikasten, *Most Splendid Failure*, pp. 124–125.

19. Blotner, *Faulkner*, vol. 1, p. 427, and Minter, *Faulkner*, p. 62.

20. Blotner, *Faulkner*, vol. 1, p. 511.

21. Ibid., pp. 455 and 542.

22. The most emotionally compelling relationships in Faulkner's prose are those between brothers and sisters. It is in part the impossibility of a meaningful consummation of such relationships—and, thus, the innate and ongoing sense of loss—that accounts for their fascination for Faulkner and for the potency of the longing that exists among siblings in his fiction. Since fusion is the end of distinctions and the end of desire, the apotheosis of desire is to long for something impossible to attain, something already lost.

23. William G. Niederland, M.D., "The Symbolic River-Sister Equation in Poetry and Folklore," *Journal of Hillside Hospital* 6 (1957): 91.

24. Bleikasten, *Most Splendid Failure*, p. 60.

25. Ibid., p. 119. Bleikasten argues, paradoxically, that Quentin's "nostalgia for lost innocence is above all the dream of a sexless life" (p. 99). He makes explicit the nature and source of the disgust that Quentin and his father share: "Woman's delicacy and suavity are a decoy; the sanctuary of her body hides an ignoble secret: the filth of sex, at once the periodically renewed promise of fecundity . . . and the threat of mortal engulfment. In Quentin's diseased imagination, the menstrual flow and 'liquid putrefaction' are confused in the same obscene streaming" (p. 100).

In several notes to his own text, Bleikasten reminds us that concern with purity, dirt, and stains such as that found in Quentin's section of the novel is characteristic of the anal phase of infantile development, and he discusses the relationship of the "central experience of loss" in the book to the dirt and stain imagery and feelings of disgust we find there. Quentin's obsessive behavior (avoiding having to know the exact time, meticulously packing and preparing for his suicide) and, in general, his attempts to "hold on" to the past rather than "letting go" of it are consistent with this interpretation. Since control is Quentin's preoccupation—as well as the basic learning task of the anal stage of development—this convergence of elements associated with the stage seems apt, even if disquieting. Ibid., pp. 222–224, notes 10, 14, and 17. My own study, of course, is also about control, Faulkner's narrative control of perceptions and, in a larger sense, of his characters' experience of the world around them.

26. Blotner, *Faulkner*, vol. 1, p. 572. Michael Millgate recognizes the importance of twilight in Faulkner's work in *The Achievement of William Faulkner* (London: Constable, 1966), p. 86.

27. According to Michel Gresset, Faulkner is like other writers in the Symbolist tradition in treating twilight as "the moment of all possible revelations." "Faulkner's 'The Hill,'" *Southern Literary Journal* 6 (Spring 1974): 12.

28. Once again, André Bleikasten and I have reached the same conclusions. He sees mourning as "a possible key," "a motif readily traced in the novels themselves." And he believes as well that *The Sound and the Fury* and *As I Lay Dying* "are novels *about* lack and loss, in which desire is always intimately bound up with death." *Most Splendid Failure*, pp. 52–53.

3. Significant Absences

1. Bergson, *Creative Evolution*, pp. 296–324.
2. Ibid., p. 306; final italics are mine.
3. Ibid.
4. The tension at the ghost's boundaries between the fluid and the permanent is another visual example of Faulkner's fascination with the effects of transience.
5. Walter J. Slatoff, *Quest for Failure: A Study of William Faulkner* (Ithaca: Cornell University Press, 1960), especially pp. 83–87, 93, 135–137, 239–265.
6. The oxymoronic structure can, of course, be a "both/and" proposition as well, but it is characteristic of Faulkner's concerns that he should prefer its negative possibilities. See ibid., pp. 122–127.
7. Clearly, such constructions also convey a sense of our inability to capture reality conceptually or linguistically, but the affect implied remains a sense of loss.
8. See especially Hirushi Hayakawa, "Negation in William Faulkner," in *Studies in English Grammar and Linguistics: A Miscellany in Honour of Takanobu Otsuka*, edited by K. Araki et al. (Tokyo: Kenkyusha Ltd., 1958), pp. 103–116.
9. Quoted in Blotner, *Faulkner*, vol. 1, pp. 531–532.
10. See note 22 to this chapter for an example.
11. Drusilla Hawk in "An Odor of Verbena" and Claude Hope in "Turnabout" are among such figures.
12. David Minter makes a similar point about Faulkner's fondness for obliquity: "those things most worth seeing, knowing, and saying can never be directly or fully seen, known, and said. But the indirection and incompletion that his descriptions stress are also useful strategies for approaching forbidden scenes, uttering forbidden words, committing dangerous acts." *Faulkner*, p. 103.
13. Faulkner's decision "to approach Caddy only by indirection" may have been, as Minter suggests, in part a technical one and in part because Faulkner believed indirection to be more "passionate." Minter, *Faulkner*, pp. 96–97. But Minter himself implies another reason we do not see Caddy directly. He suggests that, unlike her brothers, "the girl who had the courage to climb the tree would also find the courage to face change and loss" (p. 96). Faulkner would be unlikely to depict directly the consciousness of someone living courageously and without ambivalence in the face of "change and loss" because it is precisely an inability to do this that plagued him and all of his introspective protagonists. Caddy, living in a way that Faulkner admired and longed to do, would almost have *had* to remain remote, Other. Cf. Bleikasten, *Most Splendid Failure*, p. 65.

14. In *The Town* Gavin Stevens fantasizes drolly about the community's awareness of his incipient liaison with Linda, Eula Varner's daughter: "Besides, the drugstore meetings were not even a weekly affair, let alone daily, so even a whole week could pass before (1) it would occur to someone that we had not met in over a week, who (2) would immediately assume that we had something to conceal was why we had not met in over a week, and (3) the fact that we had met again after waiting over a week only proved it" (T 203).

15. See Slatoff, "The Space Between," *Quest for Failure*, pp. 128–132.

16. Minter agrees that Faulkner saw the external world as "fragmentary and unstable." But he goes on to say: "Rather than simply bemoan this fact, [Faulkner] took consolation in it; for what the mutability of the world of act and deed implied, beyond loss, was opportunity. Several years later, he described his great-grandfather as epitomizing the heroic possibilities of the real, then noted that all the Old Colonel's achievements had *faded*: 'There's nothing left in the old place, the house is gone and the plantation *boundaries*, nothing left of his work but a statue.' Seemingly as an afterthought he added that he liked 'it better that way,' suggesting that it was as both living and dying force that his great ancestor appealed to him." Minter, *Faulkner*, p. 87, emphasis mine; Minter is quoting from Robert Cantwell, "The Faulkners: Recollections of a Gifted Family," *New World Writing* 2 (1952): 300–315; reprinted in Hoffman and Vickery, eds., *William Faulkner*, p. 56. That Faulkner might really have liked "it better that way" seems doubtful, given the emotionally overdetermined role he assigns to boundaries and containers in his fictive world.

17. Responding to an interview question about Ernest Hemingway, Faulkner described his contemporary's limitations in these terms: "He never did try to get outside the boundary of what he really could do and risk failure. He did what he really could do marvelously well, first rate, but to me that is not success but failure . . . [sic] failure to me is the best." Quoted in Meriwether and Millgate, eds., *Lion in the Garden*, p. 88. A defiance of boundaries is, for Faulkner, an aspect of artistic success; the best art entails a movement into the realm of events and emotions that are themselves amorphous and ambiguous, where the artist's goal is to evoke these inexpressible experiences. Faulkner's own rhythms of flowing and control testify to his confrontation of the problem.

18. These same economic assumptions are evident as Joe Christmas pays the prostitutes to assure his autonomy, as Addie Bundren gives Anse children to "negative" or "replace" others she feels she has robbed him of, and as Quentin Compson stays the full year at Harvard to get the family's money's worth for having sold Benjy's pasture.

In a letter to Joan Williams dated September 8, 1951, Faulkner wrote: "I am too old to have to miss a girl of twenty-three years old. By now, I should have earned the right to be free of that." Quoted in Blotner, *Faulkner*, vol. 2, p. 1395.

19. Several observations in this paragraph are from Hayakawa, "Negation in William Faulkner," pp. 108–109.

20. Slatoff emphasizes the incoherence Faulkner's more intellectual characters often reveal in their interpretations of events. *Quest for Failure*, p. 148.

21. Adams writes that "this opposition between dynamic life and static word is a basic element of Faulkner's style." *Myth and Motion*, p. 106. And Bleikasten concludes that in many of Faulkner's stories garrulity "functions as an index to futility and failure, while being taciturn signals unimpaired powers to live and create." *Most Splendid Failure*, p. 27.

22. Such concepts as virginity, for example, have importance only for his male characters. They seem to find some security (or perhaps predictability) in focusing upon boundaries: codes of bravery and chivalry, the honor of one's family (birthright, chastity of one's women), and conventions of behavior (such as hunting rituals). Such codes and concepts are for the most part definitions of men's relationships with one another, with nature, and with women, and self-definitions that provide them with a sense of autonomy or identity. Women have neither an interest in defining experience in such terms nor an investment in maintaining these distinctions. Eula Varner and others like her serenely defy the masculine categories for women by being, like the goddesses of Greece, "at once corrupt and immaculate, at once virgins and the mothers of warriors and of grown men" (H 113).

23. Cf. Minter, *Faulkner*, p. 37.

24. Ibid., p. 240.

25. Consider the black brogans that threaten Joe Christmas's sense of identity (LA 313); Labove's sending of football shoes to his family (H 102–104); Moketubbe's patent-leather shoes with red heels in "Red Leaves" (CS 320–321); and Sutpen, who visualizes wealth in terms of "the man who did not even have to wear the shoes he owned" (AA 234). Blotner corroborates the evocative power of shoes for Faulkner's imagination in several anecdotes; see especially *Faulkner*, vol. 1, p. 366.

26. André Bleikasten has written: "Like memory, [odor] is a diffuse presence, a felt absence, a tantalizing intimation of being. . . . to the extent that it always has the power to evoke something other than itself, to point an absence, one might consider it a 'natural' metaphor. Small wonder, then, that the fragrance of *honeysuckle* is the most pregnant and most poignant symbol in the Quentin section [of *The Sound and the Fury*]." *Most Splendid Failure*, p. 63.

27. Although the dominant use of the trace is as a referent for some-

thing experienced in the past, it can occasionally be something anticipating the presence of an event in the future. As one example, Hightower's "odor of overplump desiccation and stale linen" is seen as a "precursor of the tomb" (LA 300). But such a usage is infrequent in Faulkner's work since his preoccupation is with the past and with loss.

28. William Faulkner, foreword to *The Faulkner Reader* (New York: Random House, Modern Library, 1954), p. ix.

29. For some psychoanalysts' observations on the restorative role of creativity, see André Green, "Le double et l'absent," *Critique* 29 (May 1973): 393–416; Melanie Klein, "Infantile Anxiety-Situations Reflected in a Work of Art and in the Creative Impulse" and "Mourning and its Relation to Manic-Depressive States," in *Contributions to Psychoanalysis, 1921–1945* (London: Hogarth Press, 1950); William G. Niederland, M.D., "Clinical Aspects of Creativity," *American Imago* 24 (1967): 6–33.

30. See Minter, *Faulkner*, p. 95: Faulkner "used the remembered as he used the actual—less to denominate lived events, relationships, and configurations, with their attendant attributes and emotions, than to objectify them and so be free to analyze and play with them. . . ."

31. Spatial patterns are especially evident in *The Sound and the Fury*, where, as Arthur Geffen points out, Quentin is described both as waiting until the end of the academic year to commit suicide in order to get "the full value of his paid-in-advance tuition" (TSAF, Appendix 411) and (in the text) as killing himself a week before the end of the year, before the boat races and while classes are still in session. The literal discrepancy is not important; what is important is the sense of a pattern being set up and not quite completed. Arthur Geffen, "Profane Time, Sacred Time, and Confederate Time in *The Sound and the Fury*," *Studies in American Fiction* 2 (1974): 175–197. Geffen discusses an interesting "day-before" pattern in the novel. A number of important dates (including those heading each section) are the day before the anniversary of significant events in Southern history. The not-quite-filling of a carefully delineated space is consistent with the modes of perception this study elaborates.

4. "The Terror of History": Faulkner's Solution

1. See especially Mircea Eliade, *Rites and Symbols of Initiation: The Mysteries of Birth and Rebirth*, translated by Willard R. Trask (New York: Harper & Row, Harper Torchbook, 1965).

2. Minter, *Faulkner*, p. xii.

3. Ibid., p. xi.

4. Mircea Eliade, *The Myth of the Eternal Return or, Cosmos and History*, translated by Willard R. Trask, Bollingen Series, no. 46 (Princeton: Princeton University Press, 1971), p. 5.

5. Consider this line from "Carcassonne": "Steed and rider thunder

on, thunder punily diminishing: a dying star upon the immensity of darkness and of silence within which, steadfast, fading, deepbreasted and grave of flank, muses the dark and tragic figure of the Earth, his mother" (CS 900).

6. An obvious example is Joe Christmas's killing of the sheep and dipping his hands into the blood to free himself from the knowledge of menstruation. When he is forced to be aware of menstruation again because it keeps him from being with Bobbie Allen, he is appalled (LA 177).

7. In *The Wild Palms* the annual celebration of Christmas is described explicitly as a renewal, but it is an ironic one, "when for seven days the rich get richer and the poor get poorer in amnesty: the whitewashing of a stipulated week leaving the page blank and pristine again for the chronicling of the fresh . . . revenge and hatred" (WP 130).

8. When the reciprocal trust between Old Ben and the hunters is broken in *Go Down, Moses*—when they believe he has "broken the rules" by killing a colt—they begin to hunt him in earnest (GDM 214).

9. The snake is a bisexual symbol, capable of representing either masculine phallic or feminine incorporative powers. Here, the snake is seen as feminine, as Faulkner's language confirms with its associations between the snake's characteristics (accursed, smell, knowledge, death) and specific anxieties he regularly attributes to the presence of women.

10. It should be noted, though, that Faulkner ultimately considered Ike a flawed figure because his detachment from life was so severe. He simply repudiated the very involvements that make life worthwhile. Faulkner continued to play fictionally with various degrees of participation in or withdrawal from life. See Minter, *Faulkner*, p. 189.

11. Bleikasten discusses the opposition represented by the two men as "furious action vs. passive suffering, aggressive masculinity vs. effeminacy, inarticulate brooding vs. febrile intellectuality." *Most Splendid Failure*, p. 37. He also observes, but does not pursue, the perverse transcendence found in the novel, alluding to Bayard's "desire to transcend finiteness through the apotheosis of a violent, self-willed death" (p. 38).

12. See Minter, *Faulkner*, pp. 99–103.

13. The word "radius" suggests once again that femininity is perceived as a containing space which, being female, threatens to envelop the male. Another character who encounters Eula, Gavin Stevens, finds the same threat implicit in her sexuality: "She simply confronted me . . . with that blue envelopment like the sea, not questioning nor waiting, as the sea itself doesn't need to question or wait but simply to be the sea" (T 92).

14. The cyclical rhythms of the female are temporal ones, the natural rhythms of life such as giving birth, and they convey her comfortableness in living in the present moment. The cyclical patterns associated

with males, however, are distinctly spatial ones, in which movement—especially circular movement—ends in a somewhat deterministic feeling of entrapment. Given the associations to the female and the male that we have seen pervading Faulkner's prose, we might conclude that the tendency of the male (including Faulkner as author and his narrators and characters) to spatialize the reality outside himself in his need to create the illusion of control is a consequence of his inability to live in the present moment and his inability to be comfortable with the temporal rhythms of life. That is to say, the male perhaps creates his own entrapment by projecting spatial patterns onto external events; instead of rhythms, he evokes rigidity and perpetuates, rather than alleviates, his anxiety about the passage of time. As the epigraph to the first chapter states, "his own flesh as well as all space was still a cage" (LA 151).

15. Cf. the descriptions of the little Italian girl in Quentin's section of *The Sound and the Fury*, who reminds him of his sister Caddy: "She just looked at me, serene and secret and chewing" (TSAF 160); "She looked at me, chewing, her eyes black and unwinking and friendly" (TSAF 162). Even at her young age, she conveys the serenity of the feminine, at home with natural rhythms.

16. Labove thinks about Eula: "He saw that she not only was not going to study, but there was nothing in books here or anywhere else that she would ever need to know, who had been born already completely equipped not only to face and combat but to overcome anything the future could invent to meet her with" (H 114).

17. Irwin, *Doubling and Incest/Repetition and Revenge*, p. 101.

18. Friedrich Nietzsche, *Thus Spoke Zarathustra*, in *The Portable Nietzsche*, translated by Walter Kaufmann (New York: Viking Press, 1954), pp. 251–252; quoted in ibid., pp. 101–102.

19. Irwin, *Doubling and Incest/Repetition and Revenge*, p. 4.

20. Examples of the latter are Boon Hogganbeck in the last scene of "The Bear" and Benjy Compson in *The Sound and the Fury*, for whom any ritual's predictability is all that matters (TSAF 399–401).

21. Not putting an appropriate boundary on the past is a negative trait for most of Faulkner's protagonists, because it makes them incapable of living healthily in the present moment. Theirs is a compulsive refusal to let go; in the elderly, however, Faulkner seems to imply and, as if in response to his own deep ambivalence toward the past, to encourage a nostalgic flowing back and forth between the two times, past *and* present, somehow less dangerous and less pathological.

22. The fact that Lucas has two strains of blood that are not battling one another does not mean that a state of perfect integration or fusion has taken place. Instead, the two bloods are seen as the "toxin" and its "anti" which have stalemated each other, that is, erased or canceled one another out. The anxiety created in Faulkner by the idea of miscegena-

tion apparently never allows him to describe it as a fully healthy or desirable phenomenon, although in Lucas we see an attempt to account for his dignity by imaginatively asserting the peaceful coexistence of these natural "enemies."

23. It is far more typical for Faulkner to assume that a crossing of boundaries that results in hybrid offspring will end in confusion and failure. In *Flags in the Dust* Jackson MacCallum tries to breed a new animal by crossing a fox ("Ethyl") with a hound ("General"). The result is a strange litter of puppies: "No two of them looked alike, and none of them looked like anything else. Neither fox nor hound; partaking of both, yet neither; and despite their soft infancy, there was about them something monstrous and contradictory and obscene" (FD 374). (Note the echoes of Shakespeare's "The Phoenix and the Turtle.") In his canine wisdom, the puppies' father rejects them: "[General] stood looking at them with fascination and bafflement and a sort of grave horror, then he gave his master one hurt, reproachful look and turned and departed, his tail between his legs" (FD 375). The adults present seem to agree with General's decision. Crossbreeding, for Faulkner, remains imaginatively disquieting.

24. See Minter, *Faulkner*, p. 177. Speaking of the very successful figure of Ratliff in *The Hamlet*, Minter writes: "More than any other protagonist Faulkner was ever to create, Ratliff balances involvement and detachment . . ." *Faulkner*, p. 182. Significantly, like the mule, Ratliff is celibate.

25. Minter, *Faulkner*, p. 67.

26. Quoted in ibid., p. 64.

27. Ibid., p. 232.

28. Ibid.

29. Quoted in Meta Carpenter Wilde and Orin Borsten, *A Loving Gentleman: The Love Story of William Faulkner and Meta Carpenter* (New York: Simon and Schuster, 1976), p. 317.

30. Minter, *Faulkner*, p. 176; Minter is quoting from William Faulkner, "Books and Things: Joseph Hergesheimer," in *William Faulkner: Early Prose and Poetry*, edited by Collins, p. 101.

31. See Wilde and Borsten, *A Loving Gentleman*, p. 244.

32. Minter, *Faulkner*, p. 116: "Of the female facility for enveloping and engulfing, [Faulkner] had become especially wary."

33. The pronoun in this quotation refers to the protagonist in "Carcassonne," but several of Faulkner's characters share the same sort of bodily awareness.

34. Minter, *Faulkner*, p. 109.

35. Ibid., pp. 162–163.

36. Ibid., p. 163.

37. Gail L. Mortimer, "The Ironies of Transcendent Love in Faulkner's *The Wild Palms*," forthcoming in *Faulkner Studies*, vol. 3.

38. Cf. William Faulkner, *Soldiers' Pay*, p. 204: "Sex and Death: the front door and the back door of the world. How indissolubly are they associated in us!"

39. Minter, *Faulkner*, pp. 20 and 21; see also p. 28.

40. Ibid., p. 64.

41. Ibid., pp. 114–116.

42. Ibid., p. 61.

43. Ibid., pp. 18 and 87.

44. Ibid., p. 93.

45. Ibid., p. 103.

46. Ibid., p. 56.

47. Gwynn and Blotner, eds., *Faulkner in the University*, p. 6.

48. Minter, *Faulkner*, p. 116; Minter is quoting from *Mosquitoes*, p. 339.

49. Minter, *Faulkner*, p. 102.

50. Quoted in Gwynn and Blotner, eds., *Faulkner in the University*, p. 65.

51. Quentin's father, Jason, says to him in *The Sound and the Fury*: "you cannot bear to think that someday it will no longer hurt you like this" (TSAF 220).

52. Minter, *Faulkner*, p. 56.

53. Ibid., p. 58.

Index

Geffen, Arthur, 144n
Getting even, motive of, 113
Gibson, Dilsey, 44
Go Down, Moses, 14–15, 98, 101–103, 115–116
Greenacre, Phyllis, 16
Gresset, Michel, 140n
Grierson, Emily, 31: and denial of loss, 1
Grimm, Percy, 27
Grove, Lena, 25, 31, 34, 38: as foil, 16, 36, 133n

Hamlet, The, 48–49, 108–110
Hemingway, Ernest, 142n
Hightower, Gail, 27, 31, 33, 104–105
Hightower, Gail (grandfather), 33–34
Hines, Eupheus (Doc), 16, 19
History, denial of, through ritual, 99
Hogganbeck, Boon, 102
Homosexual fantasy, 110
Horses, cars, planes as means of escape, 39, 49, 106
Houston, Jack, 48, 83–84
Human identity, formation of, 2–5, 13–14, 16, 47, 131–135n; and absence of needed things, 3
Husserl, Edmund, 137n

Identity theme (Lichtenstein), 4
Incest: as apotheosis of desire, 121, 128, 139n; as theme, 67–69
Indirection, 49–54, 141n
Intruder in the Dust, 116
Irwin, John, 5, 112

Jung, Carl Gustav, 25
"Justice, A," 127

Kant, Immanuel: and forms of perception, 44

Keats, John, 105, 134n
King, Roma, 58
Knight's Gambit, 28
Kohl, Linda Snopes, 85–86, 94

Labove (schoolteacher), 108–110
Lichtenstein, Heinz, 4, 132–135n
Light in August, 6, 38: androgyny in, 31–33; getting even as theme of, 85; identity as theme of, 12, 16–26; imagery in, 45; implied determinism in, 29–30, 104; women in, 17–26, 39, 66

MacCallum, Jackson, 147n
McCaslin, Buck (Uncle), 110–111
McCaslin, Buddy (Uncle), 110–111
McCaslin, Carothers, 116–117
McCaslin, Isaac (Ike), 26, 101–103, 115, 145n
McEachern, Mrs., 17, 21–22
McEachern, Simon, 20: as Calvinist, 134n
Mansion, The, 100
Marble Faun, The, 35
Mayes, Will, 55–57
Medusa, 32, 78
Millard, Rosa ("Granny"), 118
Millgate, Michael, 140n
Minter, David, 132–133n, 142n: on Faulkner and women, 121–124, 126, 127, 147n; on Faulkner's art and life, 9–11, 92, 126, 128–129, 144n; on Faulkner's childhood, 14–15; on Faulkner's obliquity, 141n; on involvement vs. detachment, 10, 39, 98, 122, 126, 136n, 147n
Miscegenation, 115–117, 120–121, 147n
Mitchell, Belle, 123
Mosquitoes: on artist as killing what he describes, 42, 46